AF248917

The Family Therapy Collections

James C. Hansen, Series Editor

Alan J. Hovestadt and Marshall Fine, Volume Editors

AN ASPEN PUBLICATION®
Aspen Publishers, Inc.
Rockville, Maryland
Royal Tunbridge Wells
1987

Library of Congress Cataloging-in-Publication Data

Family of origin therapy.

(The Family therapy collections, ISSN: 0735-9152)
"An Aspen publication."
Includes bibliographies and index.
1. Family psychotherapy. 2. Intergenerational
relations. I. Hovestadt, Alan J. II. Fine, Marshall.
III. Series. [DNLM: 1. Family Therapy. W1 FA454N /
WM430.5.F2 F198 1986]
RC488.5.F327   1986   616.89′156   86-32083
ISBN: 0-89443-621-X

The Family Therapy Collections series is indexed in *Psychological Abstracts* and the PsycINFO database

Article reprints are available from University Microfilms International, 300 North Zeeb Road, Dept. A.R.S., Ann Arbor, MI 48106.

Editorial Services: Ruth Bloom

Library of Congress Catalog Card Number: 86-32083
ISBN: 0-89443-621-X
ISSN: 0735-9152

Printed in the United States of America

1   2   3   4   5

Table of Contents

Series Preface

Family therapy collections is a quarterly publication in which topics of current and specific interest to family therapists are presented. Each volume serves as a source of information for practicing therapists by translating theoretical and research conceptualizations into practical applications. Authored by practicing professionals, the articles in each volume provide in-depth coverage of a single aspect of family therapy.

This volume concentrates on Family-of-Origin Therapy. Although nearly all family therapists adhere to systems concepts of family relationships, most therapists focus specifically on the nuclear family members. In addition to the critical events of the presenting family, a family-of-origin therapist may focus on three generations of the family evolutionary patterns. Family behaviors derive meaning in relation to the sociocultural history of the family. By knowing the life cycle transactions, the therapist can place the present situation in perspective with the family pattern. Methods of family of origin may be applied as the therapist's general approach to change behavior or as a technique to increase understanding of the family background. This volume presents various concepts of family-of-origin therapy and numerous examples of the applications.

Alan Hovestadt and Marshall Fine are the volume editors. Alan J. Hovestadt is Professor and Chair of the Department of Counselor Education and Counseling Psychology at Western Michigan University. Formerly he was Professor and Clinical Director of Family Therapy Education at East Texas State University. Hovestadt received his EdD in Counselor Education with a concentration in Family Therapy at Northern Illinois University. His areas of research and publication include family-of-origin issues, family therapy education, and supervision. He maintains a private practice and provides consulting to a variety of institutions and organizations on organizational development and human relations. Hovestadt is a Fellow and Approved Supervisor in the American Association for Marriage and Family Therapy.

Marshall Fine is an Assistant Professor in the Department of Family Studies at the University of Guelph where he is involved in the education, training, and supervision of family therapy students. His professional pursuits include intergenerational relationships, epistemology, and well functioning families.

Please note that a list of all previous volumes, as well as future ones, in the FAMILY THERAPY COLLECTION appears following the index.

James C. Hansen
Series Editor

Preface

Family-of-origin therapy has been conducted in some form or another since the beginning of the family therapy movement. With time, the theories underscoring family-of-origin therapy have become more clearly explicated and diverse. Few family therapists would dispute the impact of the family-of-origin experience on the thoughts and behavior of offspring. Therapists would, of course, dispute the necessity of using family-of-origin therapy to deal with the influences of these early learnings. Family-of-origin therapists, however, are convinced that one of the best and most powerful ways of modifying these influences on present behavior is to actively work these issues through, with, or in light of, the family of origin.

Although family-of-origin therapy has a long history relative to the family therapy movement, the literature on the subject has generally not addressed new or emerging family problems. For example, how do family-of-origin therapists deal with family violence, sexual dysfunction, and cultural issues? In addition, little literature exists comparing and contrasting the number of family-of-origin approaches.

The present volume has been written to address these and other issues related to family-of-origin therapy. This volume is not meant as the definitive foundation for family-of-origin therapy. It is, however, an exploration of the topic in a broad and systematic manner.

S. Allen Wilcoxon, an Assistant Professor and Coordinator of Community/ Agency Counselor Education at the University of Alabama, presents a concise overview of the intergenerational concepts used by various family-of-origin therapists. This chapter forms the foundation for the volume by reviewing the basic concepts used throughout the volume.

Marshall Fine and Alan J. Hovestadt explore the nature of family-of-origin therapy, comparing and contrasting the approaches of the leading figures in the family-of-origin field.

James Gladstone is a Social Worker and Researcher at the Baycrest Centre for Geriatric Care, Toronto, Ontario. His chapter outlines areas in which intergenerational participation would be useful in the therapeutic process. He notes that family therapists too often forget that other generation family members might be quite helpful in the therapy process.

James H. Bray, Texas Women's University, Houston, and Donald S. Williamson, Houston Family Institute, have written a chapter on assessment of intergenerational family relationships. They outline the process of assessment within the clinical interview and discuss the use of the *Personal Authority in the Family System* questionnaire.

Barbara Pressman, Wilfrid Laurier University, Waterloo, Ontario, describes the use of family-of-origin therapy in the treatment of wife abuse. Her unique program uses family-of-origin therapy as well as other treatment approaches, to deal with this most complex issue.

Claude A. Guldner, Professor-in-Charge, Child and Family Services and Research Unit, University of Guelph, Guelph, Ontario, describes the use of family-of-origin therapy within a sex therapy framework. He demonstrates specifically how family-of-origin therapy can be used to deal with sexual dysfunction.

Joseph R. Morris, Department of Counselor Education and Counseling Psychology, Western Michigan University, Kalamazoo, explores the issue of family-of-origin therapy with Black Families. He points to the unique features of the American Black family-of-origin relationships.

Milo F. Benningfield, Private Practice, Southwest Family Institute, Dallas, addresses the issue of training and supervision in family-of-origin therapy. He outlines the unique features regarding supervision within the family-of-origin therapy framework.

William T. Anderson, Department of Family and Consumer Studies, Texas Woman's University, Denton, completes the volume with a chapter on the graduate teaching of family-of-origin therapy. This chapter will be of interest to educators who wish to develop a whole course on the subject, or who want to deal more thoroughly with the topic within a more broadly based course in family therapy.

Alan J. Hovestadt
Marshall Fine
Volume Editors

1. Perspectives in Intergenerational Concepts

S. Allen Wilcoxon, EdD
*Assistant Professor and Coordinator of Community
Agency Counselor Education
University of Alabama
Tuscaloosa, Alabama*

While it is impossible to determine the extent to which early life experiences affect later life functioning, it is equally impossible to deny the impact of these experiences. Many aspects of human behavior (e.g., preferences for social interactions, behavioral limits, moral values, personal and social expectations, sex role identity, parenting, and citizenship) seem to be linked invariably to significant events that transpire in an individual's early years. More often than not, these aspects of human behavior seem to originate in early life experiences within the family environment.

In this regard, Framo (1981) stated that "of all the forces that impinge upon people (culture, society, work, neighborhood, friends, etc.), the family by far has the greatest imprinting influence" (p. 133). Generally speaking, the emotional atmosphere, interpersonal relationship patterns, role related behaviors and expectations, and rules of order that characterize relationships within the family in which an individual is reared have been defined as family-of-origin experiences (Bowen, 1976, 1978; Framo, 1976). Relationships with extended family members who do not reside in the home of the original family add further complexity to the notion of sustained influences across generational boundaries.

Conceptual notions concerning intergenerational influences have been found in the literature for a considerable time. Writers in the field of human studies and intervention have noted the powerful influence of the original family (e.g., Carl Rogers and Alfred Adler). Even the apparently "ahistorical"

1

model of social learning theory lends support to the notion that early life patterns of reinforcement, particularly those within the family, establish preferences for seeking and providing reinforcement in contemporary social and familial settings. Still, these and other models of human behavior seem to approach the historical and contemporary effects of intergenerational relationships as simple extensions of their theoretical postulates. In contrast, other theoretical models of family therapy feature a central focus on the intergenerational influences of the family system. Proponents of these models have devoted considerably greater attention to the rich, yet complex, nature of intergenerational relationships and their influences on current behavior.

CLASSIC PERSPECTIVES

In any examination of the developments in intergenerational family therapy, the contrasts between contemporary theoretical models and their precursors are quite obvious.

Freud

As with most "beginning" discussions of human behavior, the classic literature regarding intergenerational relationships has its genesis in the works of Freud. The focus of Freud's writings on intergenerational relationships during the earliest years of life centers on two particularly cogent issues: (1) the mechanistic, biological motivation for stage-specific behaviors of psychosexual development and (2) the static, fixed nature of early life experiences that, unless otherwise negated, are alleged to influence personality *in exactly the same manner* across time (Hall, 1954).

Although Freud found validity in the notion that interpersonal relationships contribute to personality development and human behavior, he noted that an individual's instinctive biological urges are the principal forces that drive the individual to seek interpersonal exchanges. Furthermore, Freud emphasized the importance of the gratification of biological needs at crucial stages of personality development (Freud, 1915). Still, the central focus of this aspect of Freudian theory is on the fulfillment of individual biological needs within the social realm. Adjunctive to this notion was Freud's belief that the familial environment, particularly the mother-child relationship, determines to some extent whether these individual needs are satisfactorily met. Clearly, this idea is a precursor to the more contemporary view of family systems.

Freud's belief that early life experiences can affect individual personality development in a manner that is essentially static and changeless led to his premises concerning "fixation" or retardation in the developmental process. In this way, he explained the resilience of innumerable later life, neurotic behaviors in adults (Hall, 1954). For some subsequent practitioners and writers, however, Freud's fixation postulate appeared to be without merit. Their skepticism resulted in the more contemporary notion of dynamic, system-regulated relationships among family members (Speer, 1970). Classic Freudian theory was further modified by neo-Freudians (e.g., H. S. Sullivan) who emphasized more fully social interaction as a significant factor in individual development.

The Freudian traditions have contributed greatly to contemporary practices in individual and systemic intervention. From these roots came the tenets of object relations theory, the next phase of development in the classic perspectives of intergenerational family therapy.

Fairbairn

Elaborating on Freud's psychodynamic perspective, Fairbairn (1954) focused on the effects of familial interactions on individual personality development. His disagreement with Freud's ideas about biological drives and Freud's relatively narrow view of the parent-child relationship led to Fairbairn's object relations model of personality development.

At its most simplistic level of conceptualization, the object relations perspective emphasizes the importance of parental acceptance or rejection of a child's behaviors. In this view, parents are in a real sense the "objects" of the child's affection and attention (Mallouk, 1982). Fairbairn surmised that the child internalizes familial interactions, both satisfactory and unsatisfactory, as psychological representations of early life experiences. These retained experiences, or "introjects," serve as reminders of the positive and negative aspects of the parent-child relationship, thereby influencing the child's cognitive and affective functioning, as well as the child's perceptions of self and others.

Fairbairn (1954) observed that parental introjects are highly subjective and typically immune to straightforward confrontation. He postulated that the child's manner of coping with negative introjects (e.g., denial, projection, anger, withdrawal) quickly becomes part of the child's personality and style of social interaction. He further speculated that introjects are resilient guides for perceiving self and others (not entirely dissimilar to Freud's notions of fixation). Finally, Fairbairn noted that, in later life situations that are similar to those earlier situations in which negative introjects were internalized, an adult perceives and reacts to others (e.g., spouse, friends) in the same manner that he or she had perceived and reacted to parents in earlier years.

Some practitioners have embraced and elaborated Fairbairn's object relations model, further developing its intrapsychic premises (Mallouk, 1982; Stewart, Peters, Marsh, & Peters, 1975). While these practitioners applauded

Fairbairn's ideas for going beyond the restrictiveness of Freudian psychology, others expressed dissatisfaction with the emphasis on individual development and the implication that the individual cannot break free of the bonds of a behavioral/perceptual style established in the early years of life (Framo, 1981). The apparent permanence of early life introjects seemed to cast a shadow over the likelihood of positive change for later life relationships.

Like those who adhered to Freudian or neo-Freudian theory, those who adhered to the object relations approach believed that an individual can alter established patterns (i.e., introjects) by recounting and overcoming traumas with a trained professional *in the absence of others*. They believed that hope for emotional freedom stems from changes within the individual that must then be introduced to significant others. Recognition of the power of the family system was not at the core of these classic perspectives. At this point, it was clear that therapists who wanted to adopt an intergenerational perspective had come to a crossroad; they must either progress along quasi-Freudian paths or establish new lines of thought and accompanying interventions.

CONTEMPORARY PERSPECTIVES

Despite apparent points of divergence, contemporary intergenerational perspectives of family therapy feature some common threads. Of key significance in this regard is their focus on the continuous influence of the intergenerational family system. These models purport that, while early life experiences are significant, current difficulties are dynamic in nature, rather than the static emotional imprints of days gone by.

A second shared tenet is the notion that change can and should be accomplished by familial intervention rather than by isolated individual psychotherapy. Thus, most current applications of intergenerational therapy stress systemic intervention as a viable means of effecting and sustaining desired changes.

Finally, contemporary perspectives on intergenerational family therapy suggest that difficulties and dysfunctions in relationships across generations are frequently replicated in subsequent intergenerational relationships, thereby adding to the complexity and potential trauma for members of those family systems. This process appears to multiply the problems that new generations must deal with, as well as the difficulties that therapists encounter in introducing desired changes.

Framo

In many ways, the approaches to intergenerational family intervention employed by Framo bridge the gap between traditional psychoanalytical models and systemic models of therapy. Framo's earliest attempts to embrace both models of intervention occurred in his work with adolescent inpatients in psychiatric settings (Framo, 1965). The high rate of recidivism among adolescents who had been discharged to return to their families after seemingly successful treatment led him to suspect the influence of the family environment. His inclusion of family members in sessions with adolescent inpatients quickly confirmed his suspicions that the family system, particularly the parents, hold the key to more meaningful treatment and more sustained success. "Seen in the context of the family, heretofore incomprehensible symptoms of the patient became decoded and made sense" (Framo, 1979, p. 990).

Acknowledging the significance of intrapsychic processes, Framo (1965) contended that these processes are sustained by the family environment rather than simply by the recollections and/or established patterns developed by individual members. He maintained that artifacts of parents' family-of-origin experiences are frequently the basis for the discordant behaviors of their children. In this regard, Framo (1981) stated that "the greatest gift that a couple can give to their children is a viable, marriage relationship based upon each parent's having a strong sense of self" (p. 134).

Although his work with entire families has been widely recognized, Framo's principal contribution to family therapy has been his use of the families of origin in treating couples with marital difficulties. Framo (1976) observed that couples must free themselves from the emotional bonds of their families of origin in order to establish the primacy of their marital relationship. He further contended that marital difficulties are essentially elaborations of problems that the spouses had in relationships with their original families. His "family-of-origin sessions," in which each spouse participates in family therapy with members of his or her family of origin, allow reconstructive changes in the spouse's relationships with these family members; these changes may then be infused into the current nuclear family of the distressed spouse (Framo, 1976). Framo has also advocated that discordant spouses participate in marital group therapy, noting that the dynamics of such groups can offer support, confrontation, enlightenment, and other experiences not otherwise afforded via conventional conjoint marital therapy (Framo, 1973).

Boszormenyi-Nagy

In his intergenerational perspective, Boszormenyi-Nagy focused on the "dialectic" nature of interpersonal relationships across and within generational boundaries. He posited that the affinity of human beings for relationships with others causes them to establish and sustain consistent patterns in interpersonal relationships (Boszormenyi-Nagy, 1966). Dialectic interactions typically feature complementary elements of superiority and inferiority in relationships between family members. For example, ascribed roles frequently denote inferior or superior status within family systems. Thus, a family member may have an ascribed, inferior role (e.g., scapegoat) or superior role (e.g., parent-ified child) that appreciably affects his or her self-concept, social expectations, vocational choices, and innumerable other life variables (Boszormenyi-Nagy & Spark, 1973). In addition, because family members desire exaggerated emotional closeness, a symbiotic togetherness may develop to insulate the family system from the threat of internal or external sources of change.

Complementary roles established in early life experiences may serve as the basis for later life behaviors and expectations. In this regard, Boszormenyi-Nagy and Spark (1973) observed that

> the struggle for all adults is to balance the old relationships with the new: to continually integrate the relationship with early important persons with the involvement and committedness with current relationships, namely one's mate and children. (p. 217)

Boszormenyi-Nagy (1976) speculated that these struggles result principally from unconscious motivations or desires by individual family members.

Boszormenyi-Nagy noted an interesting artifact of the model of dialectic relationships: family members seem to tabulate the emotional investments exchanged. He speculated that family members expect the instances of ascribed inferiority to balance the instances of ascribed superiority within the system and demand loyalty from other family members until such a balance is achieved. These obligatory loyalties introduce and sustain feelings of guilt, anger, or similarly intense emotions. Furthermore, such obligations may extend across two- or even three-generation boundaries. For example, a parent who makes sacrifices for a child may expect similar sacrifices from the child when he or she becomes an adult. In the event that this adult is incapable or unwilling to fulfill such obligations, the task of balancing the emotional investment may be passed to the grandchild(ren) in the family system, who may experience considerable confusion as a result.

Boszormenyi-Nagy's perspective has not been as widely accepted as many of the other contemporary applications of intergenerational family therapy. Perhaps this stems from the difficulty of establishing and measuring success in therapy outcomes.

Bowen

Like Framo, Bowen seems to encompass elements of both psychoanalytical and systemic intervention in his perspective. Bowen's model of intergenerational theory and intervention seems to be one of the most fully developed and, consequently, has received a great deal of attention.

At the heart of Bowen's model are two intrapersonal variables: anxiety and self-integration. Anxiety is principally related to adaptability and emotional robustness (Bowen, 1976); dysfunction characteristically promotes anxiety, the fear of anxiety, or both. Anxiety is generally a barometer of the degree to which an individual has achieved self-integration as evidenced by characteristics such as autonomy, intimacy, and assertiveness within the family system (Kerr, 1981). Bowen (1978) observed that self-integration is directly related to emotional autonomy, or *self-differentiation*. The degree of self-differentiation is the basis for a variety of interlocking concepts that define Bowen's model of relationships within and across generations of a family system.

Bowen (1976) noted that the single most stable emotional unit within a family is a *triangle*, a means of relating to others in which two family members triangulate another. Triangulation typically occurs when two people are unable or unwilling to address the anxiety or tension that exists in their relationship and channel those tensions toward the third, triangulated person. This tactic reduces interpersonal anxiety, but increases intrapersonal anxiety because of fear that the triangle will dissolve and the unpleasant tension will reappear. In this way, individuals become entangled in the triangle, which thus reduces their separateness or differentiation (Kerr, 1981).

Bowen (1978) maintained that a family system typically features a number of interrelated triangles. Thus, one family member may be triangulated by two other family members in one situation, while simultaneously joining with another family member to triangulate still another in a second situation. Familial triangles frequently cut across two or three generations, causing envy, anger, or emotional withdrawal. Bowen noted that these emotions are particularly evident when an individual who was triangulated by his or her parents and/or siblings within the family of origin is later triangulated by a parent and a child from his or her own nuclear family. The atmosphere in which these interrelated triangles occur is called the *nuclear family emotional system* and the process through which the replications may occur is known as the *multigenerational transmission process*.

Dysfunction within the nuclear family is frequently manifested by marital conflict, dysfunction in one spouse, or impairment of one or more children. Bowen (1978) maintained that the *family projection process* produces these symptoms within the nuclear family emotional system. Bowen noted that, when dysfunctional patterns are replicated, the degrees of self-differentiation tend to decrease with each passing generation, resulting in psychosis in at least one family member after 8 to 10 generations of transmission. The goal of therapy, according to those practitioners who accept Bowen's thorough and extensive model of intergenerational family functioning, is quite simple: to break free of the multigenerational influences that impede self-differentiation.

Some practitioners have criticized the nebulous nature of Bowen's concepts and goals for those receiving therapy based on his model (e.g., Hansen & L'Abate, 1982). The Bowenian perspective, however, is one of the more widely discussed and accepted examples of contemporary intergenerational family therapy.

Williamson

One of the most compelling contemporary applications of the intergenerational perspective is Williamson's notion of personal authority in the family system (PAFS). This model begins with the notions that each family has an intergenerational hierarchy and that systemic resilience sustains this hierarchy indefinitely (Williamson, 1981). The hierarchy denotes a position of inferiority for offspring and requires, by implicit and/or explicit communications, their submission to those in authority positions in order to sustain the integrity (i.e., balance) of the family system.

Williamson (1982a) noted that, for children and adolescents, family hierarchical boundaries provide necessary structures for decision making, discipline, nurturing, and similar parenting activities. This hierarchical structure should become obsolete, however, for adolescents and young adults who are attempting to establish self-directedness and autonomy from the family of origin. Hence, elimination of the intergenerational hierarchical boundaries and the associated superior-inferior relationships becomes an important phase of personal and systemic development. Williamson (1982b) observed that adults must establish a "peerism" relationship with their parents in order to achieve legitimate autonomy and intimacy among family members. Unless they establish a relationship based on peerism, their relationships with their original family may be based on intimidation and fear of losing emotional support (Williamson, 1982b).

An obvious artifact of fixed intergenerational hierarchical boundaries is the impact that such relationships may have on the children in the third generation (1982b). For middle generation adults, the dual roles of parent and child may give rise to resentment toward their parents, replications of their original families' intimidation within their own nuclear families, and a variety of other dysfunctional, counterproductive patterns of relationships within the family system.

Williamson's notion of PAFS is one of the more recent advances in intergenerational perspectives on family therapy. Much like Bowen, Williamson seems to view autonomy as an essential component of personal development. He also seems to support the view of Framo and Boszormenyi-Nagy that entanglement in a web of difficulties from the family of origin may impede personal growth and honest intimacy within the family system.

CONCLUSION

It is important to keep in mind that intergenerational models rarely feature the precision often noted in other approaches to marital and family therapy. Some practitioners may find this lack of precision to be a glaring liability. Others may feel that the rich opportunities for exposing and examining intergenerational relationships are worth the lack of precision. In either case, it seems that the well-prepared student, educator, practitioner, or researcher would do well to consider intergenerational influences as a viable, dynamic force in providing marital and family therapy.

REFERENCES

Boszormenyi-Nagy, I. (1966). From family therapy to a psychology of relationships: Fictions of the individual and fictions of the family. *Comprehensive Psychiatry, 7,* 408–423.

Boszormenyi-Nagy, I. (1976). Behavior change through family change. In A. Burton (Ed.), *What makes behavior change possible?* (pp. 227–258). New York: Brunner/Mazel.

Boszormenyi-Nagy, I., & Spark, G. (1973). *Invisible loyalties: Reciprocity in intergenerational family therapy.* New York: Harper & Row.

Bowen, M. (1976). Family therapy and family group therapy. In D.H. Olson (Ed.), *Treating relationships.* (pp. 219–274). Lake Mills, IA: Graphic Publishing.

Bowen, M. (1978). *Family therapy in clinical practice.* New York: Jason Aronson.

Fairbairn, W.R. (1954). *An object relations theory of the personality.* New York: Basic Books.

Framo, J. (1965). Rationale and techniques of intensive family therapy. In I. Boszormenyi-Nagy & J. Framo (Eds.), *Intensive family therapy* (pp. 143–212). New York: Harper & Row.

Framo, J. (1973). Marriage therapy in a couples group. In D.A. Block (Ed.), *Techniques of family psychotherapy: A primer* (pp. 87–97). New York: Grune & Stratton.

Framo, J. (1976). Family of origin as a therapeutic resource for adults in marital and family therapy: You can and should go home. *Family Process, 15,* 193–210.

Framo, J. (1979). Family theory and therapy. *American Psychologist, 34,* 988–992.

Framo, J. (1981). Marital therapy with sessions with family of origin. In A.S. Gurman & D.P. Kniskern (Eds.), *Handbook of family therapy* (pp. 133–158). New York: Brunner/Mazel.

Freud, S. (1915). *General introduction to psychoanalysis.* New York: Liveright.

Hall, C.S. (1954). *A primer of Freudian psychology.* Cleveland, OH. World Publishing.

Hansen, J., & L'Abate, L. (1982). *Approaches to family therapy.* New York: Macmillan.

Kerr, M.E. (1981). Family systems theory and therapy. In A.S. Gurman & D.P. Kniskern (Eds.), *Handbook of family therapy* (pp. 226–266). New York: Brunner/Mazel.

Mallouk, T. (1982). The interpersonal context of object relations: Implications for family therapy. *Journal of Marital and Family Therapy, 8,* 429–441.

Speer, D.C. (1970). Family systems: Morphostasis and morphogenesis, or "Is homeostasis enough?" *Family Process, 9,* 259–278.

Stewart, R., Peters, T., Marsh, S., & Peters, M. (1975). An object-relations approach to psychotherapy with marital couples, families, and children. *Family Process, 14,* 161–178.

Williamson, D.S. (1981). Personal authority via termination of the intergenerational hierarchical boundary: A "new" stage in the family life cycle. *Journal of Marital and Family Therapy, 7,* 441–452.

Williamson, D.S. (1982a). Personal authority via termination of the intergenerational hierarchical boundary: Part II. The consultation process and the therapeutic method. *Journal of Marital and Family Therapy, 8,* 23–37.

Williamson, D.S. (1982b). Personal authority via termination of the intergenerational hierarchical boundary: Part III. Personal authority defined, and the power of play in the change process. *Journal of Marital and Family Therapy, 8,* 309–323.

2. What Is Family-of-Origin Therapy?

Marshall Fine, EdD
Assistant Professor
Department of Family Studies
University of Guelph
Guelph, Ontario

Alan J. Hovestadt, EdD
Professor and Chair
Department of Counselor Education and Counseling Psychology
Western Michigan University
Kalamazoo, Michigan

Differences in home decorations, in political statements, and even in car bumper stickers make it clear that people "like" to distinguish themselves, to express what they stand for and how they are unique and different from others. In that sense, people "are" because of the distinctions that they make between themselves and others (Keeney, 1983).

According to family-of-origin therapists, people who are unable to distinguish or differentiate themselves from other people may become disturbed (Bowen, 1978), especially when those "other people" are their parents. Therefore, family-of-origin therapists are interested in helping individuals make clear distinctions between themselves and their parents. Only when individuals achieve "equitability" (Williamson, 1982b), equalization of power, or the establishment of "peerhood" with their parents can they feel comfortable making such distinctions and changing their statements, behaviors, and relationships with people, especially those people with whom they are intimate.

Family therapists, too, are continually making distinctions (Keeney, 1983). It is often easy to blur the meanings of particular concepts or approaches within family therapy, as demonstrated by the debate regarding the meaning of family therapy (Fine, 1984; Gurman, 1984). While some professionals may think that the distinctions made among the various family therapy approaches have a disintegrating and polarizing effect on the field, integration and union can take place only when the distinctions are clear. Thus, a consensual understanding of the nature of family-of-origin therapy can serve as a foundation for its integration into the family therapy field.

In order to provide an understanding of family-of-origin therapy, this article explores a number of areas in which this therapeutic approach can be distinguished. The differences between psychoanalytic therapy and family-of-origin therapy are outlined. Next, the use of the term "family-of-origin" therapy is clarified. The family-of-origin therapist's view of therapy, the foci and techniques, the timing, the use of parents, and the length of family-of-origin therapy are other areas that are examined.

PSYCHOANALYTICAL THERAPY VS. FAMILY-OF-ORIGIN THERAPY

There are inevitable similarities between psychoanalytical therapy and family-of-origin therapy, as there are among many approaches to family therapy. For example, the focus for both approaches is quite definitely historical. Both psychoanalysts and family-of-origin therapists are interested in, and convinced of, the potency of family-of-origin experiences. Both groups of professionals view insights gained from explorations of these experiences as therapeutic, although psychoanalysts rely more heavily on such insights.

Prior to explicating the differences between the two, it is important to note that many family therapy focused psychoanalysts have combined elements of systems theory with psychoanalytical thinking (Nichols, 1984). Indeed, Nichols (1984) includes therapists such as Framo and Boszormenyi-Nagy in his section on psychoanalytically based family therapists. Although the authors do not dispute this categorization, they tend to believe that Framo, for example, is more interactionally than intrapsychically focused in his actual therapy work. Boszormenyi-Nagy, like Framo, does not abandon the intrapsychic point of view, though he focuses his therapeutic efforts on relational determinants among family members (Boszormenyi-Nagy & Ulrich, 1981).

Classic psychoanalysts differ from family-of-origin therapists in their identification of the client. The former consider the identified individual patient to be the primary client and do not typically invite others to participate in the therapeutic process (Headley, 1977; Nichols, 1984). Indeed, a number of psychoanalytical therapists believe that the presence of other family members in the therapy room contaminates the development of transference to the therapist (Segraves, 1982). Psychoanalytical marital therapists, for example, generally prefer other approaches, such as consecutive therapy with the same spouse, concurrent therapy with the same therapist, or concurrent therapy with collaborating, but different therapists (Nadelson & Paolino, 1978). In contrast, family-of-origin therapists work with a marital couple together (Bowen, 1978; Framo, 1981) or with as many family members as appears appropriate to the problem (Boszormenyi-Nagy & Ulrich, 1981; Headley,

1977; Kramer, 1985). In essence, family-of-origin therapists are likely to view the relationship or the family as the client.

Although both psychoanalytical and family-of-origin therapists appear to be cognitively based, the former tend to be more satisfied with intellectual resolutions of problems. Psychoanalytically oriented family therapists encourage their clients to express internally the repressed impulses that originated in family-of-origin experiences (Nichols, 1984). Family-of-origin therapists, however, urge their clients to work through their problems in a more active and external way (e.g., by visiting their parents or asking their parents to attend a few therapy sessions). They want their clients to work out any object relations disturbances or distorted family-of-origin relationships in the context of their existing relationships.

FAMILY-OF-ORIGIN THERAPY: AN APPROPRIATE TERM?

The literature does not appear to delineate the distinctions, if any, among family-of-origin therapy, transgenerational therapy, and intergenerational therapy. If such distinctions do exist, they do so in the domain of semantics rather than in the domain of therapy.

The term *family-of-origin therapy* perhaps implies a more specific target than do the terms *transgenerational therapy* and *intergenerational therapy*. By definition, family-of-origin therapy appears to focus on two generations—parents and their adult children. Transgenerational therapy and intergenerational therapy, on the other hand, tend to connote at least three generations, according to many theorists who use the terms (Boszormenyi-Nagy & Spark, 1973; Kramer, 1985). In their writing on personal authority in the family system, however, Bray and Williamson (1987) tend to discuss intergenerational therapy with the more narrow two-generation focus.

Although the two-generation distinction of family-of-origin therapy may seem limiting, therapists who practice any form of "historical" family therapy generally have at least a three-generation outlook in their practice or theory regarding family functioning. Thus, the terms *family-of-origin therapy, transgenerational therapy,* and *intergenerational therapy* are essentially interchangeable, at least in describing the attitude that historically based therapists maintain with families. While the terms *intergenerational* or *transgenerational* may more accurately describe the overall outlook of therapists who are proponents of this type of approach, however, most therapists deal more often with the parent-adult child system (e.g., Bowen, 1978; Bray & Williamson, 1987; Framo, 1981). Therefore, the term *family-of-origin therapy* more accurately describes the contemporary therapeutic work.

FAMILY-OF-ORIGIN THERAPY: AN APPROACH OR A TECHNIQUE?

It is possible to view family-of-origin therapy (FOT) in at least two ways. Some therapists focus primarily and consistently on family-of-origin issues throughout the therapeutic process, as they consider this approach the logical outcome of their theoretical or epistemological base. Others use family-of-origin therapy when "appropriate" and/or at specific points in the therapy process. Kramer (1985) would be concerned that the therapist must meet the family where they are, prior to dealing with family-of-origin therapy. Pressman (1987) regularly focuses on family-of-origin issues when working with wife abuse, though she does not necessarily maintain this focus throughout the therapeutic process. Guldner (1987), would see family-of-origin therapy as necessary when dealing with certain sexual issues. Such therapists, however, consider family-of-origin therapy a vital phase of therapy in specific cases. For these therapists, family-of-origin therapy has a particular purpose, although it does not become an end in itself.

Still other therapists use "techniques" normally associated with family-of-origin therapy in the process of therapy, although they do not focus on historical issues and, therefore, are not considered family-of-origin therapists. For example, many therapists use a genogram to increase their understanding of a client's family background; in essence, they use the genogram as an assessment tool (McGoldrick & Gerson, 1985), not as a way of approaching therapy.

Foci and Techniques of Family-of-Origin Therapy

There is some question about whether the term *techniques* is an appropriate description for the activities of family-of-origin therapists, since many family-of-origin therapists appear more concerned with process than with specific symptom or problem relief. However, strategies have been developed around certain focuses that appear to be predominant in the writings of family-of-origin therapists.

Perhaps the most obvious technique or tool in family-of-origin therapy is the genogram (Bowen, 1978), which allows the therapist to visualize and operationalize intergenerational relationships. Using the genogram with a family, the therapist can elicit specific and relevant information, particularly concerning relationship patterns and pivotal events across the generations. It has a myriad of other uses (McGoldrick & Gerson, 1985) from which therapists who have adopted many different approaches can benefit.

Many family-of-origin therapists focus on detriangulating the adult child from the family of origin. Although this is not itself a "technique," it involves technical operations. Bowen (1978) planned and coached clients for "home" visits in which they were to attempt to stay clear of the family's emotional system and remain detriangulated. Framo (1975) and Headley (1977) used in-session visits with the family-of-origin members to help accomplish similar goals. These practitioners developed ways to prepare their clients for a family-of-origin session and ways to conduct such sessions. Williamson (1978) developed techniques by which adult offspring can "take care of business," even if the parents are no longer alive.

Differentiation (Bowen, 1978), or "leaving home" (Williamson, 1981), is linked to triangulation and is another focus/technique of family-of-origin therapy. Bowen (1978) noted three steps in the process of differentiation in therapy:

1. The client moves toward differentiation or autonomy.
2. The family reacts by trying to pull the client back into the emotional system.
3. The client prepares to resist the family's effort to reestablish his or her former way of functioning within the family.

Another technique used in the process of differentiation is the use of the *I* position (Bowen, 1978; Kramer, 1985). By encouraging clients to use *I*, the therapist entices them to take more responsibility for their behavior. This has the effect of clarifying the distinction between self and others, which, of course, leads to differentiation (Williamson, 1981).

Williamson (1982b) developed a rationale for the use of play and absurdity in family-of-origin work to increase the personal authority (differentiation) of the client. Although uniquely Williamson, his style is reminiscent of Whitaker's sense of the banal and absurd. Williamson (1982b) suggested that

> Intergenerational change requires the anaesthetic and the psychological leverage of humor, and heightened sense of the absurdity of all things human. A consultation style which relates playfully to the client teaches him or her to relate playfully to the previous generation. (p. 313)

Within the atmosphere that he wanted to create, Williamson developed a number of "moves" designed to accentuate absurdity and to challenge the clients' steps toward "equitability" with their parents.

The reconnection of emotional cut-offs is another focus of family-of-origin therapy (Bowen, 1978; Kramer, 1985). Although a main goal of therapy is to help individuals differentiate self from others, family-of-origin therapists are convinced that the continuation of emotional cut-offs is not beneficial for adults or their families of origin. Indeed, Williamson (1981) stated that "to be out of the emotional field of the family is to be dead, or at least to be dead-to-the-family" (p. 446). Well-differentiated contact with the family of origin makes it possible to establish a balance across the generations (Boszormenyi-Nagy & Spark, 1973; Kramer, 1985). It is assumed that, once an individual is able to detriangulate and differentiate from the family of origin, all family members will make adjustments that will lead to relatedness on a new, more beneficial level. Williamson (1981) suggests that intimacy may be established with the family of origin, when, and only when, the individual is differentiated, and is free and not obliged to choose intimacy with the parents.

Timing of Family-of-Origin Therapy

Although, to a historically or psychodynamically based therapist, family-of-origin therapy may be indicated in many instances of family disruption, some therapists believe that the timing of family-of-origin therapy is crucial to its success. Bowen (1978), for example, noted that his family systems therapy is unlikely to be effective during a family crisis. Similarly, Kramer (1985), commented that families who are experiencing a crisis may not understand the relevance of family-of-origin work until the crisis has been dealt with appropriately. She suggested that family-of-origin therapy is most useful during the middle phases of treatment, "where the goal is growth and differentiation for each member" (p. 70). According to Kramer, factors that may be useful in making a decision to use family-of-origin therapy include the relationship of the existing problem to the family of origin, the availability of other methods to solve the problem quickly, and the ability of the therapist to provide a safe environment for family members to examine unexplored past issues.

Williamson (1981) suggested that family-of-origin therapy may not be totally beneficial for clients who have not yet reached their fourth decade of life. He postulated that a clear differentiation from the family of origin cannot really be achieved earlier because the individual needs time to

- establish a separate social intimacy network
- experience financial responsibility for self and others
- deal with sexual gender identity, romantic myths of life, and children
- develop genuine compassion for his or her parents as people

When the relationship between adult clients and their parents is very unstable, Headley (1977) proposed three criteria that should be met before the parents are asked to participate in a therapy session: (1) the establishment of a trusting, supportive relationship between the client and the therapist; (2) an agreement between the client and the therapist about which family-of-origin issues are the problematic ones so that the session will have a specific focus; and (3) a clear understanding on the part of the client that the family-of-origin session can be unpredictable. Unless these criteria are met, emotionality is likely to interfere with therapy. Pressman (1987), however, appears to use family-of-origin therapy successfully when a certain amount of emotionality and anxiety can be expected.

Participation of the Parents

There are two primary views regarding the involvement of the parents/ grandparents in the treatment process. Some professionals, such as Headley (1977), Framo (1981), and Williamson (1982a), consider the eventual atten- dance of the parents/grandparents important to the therapy process. Headley (1977), for example, stated that

> to include the original childhood family members in the therapeutic process is an effective means for the adult patient to resolve old family conflicts and to gain new perceptions of his relationship to that original family. (p. 13)

Framo (1981) stated that "dealing with the real, external figures [the parents] seems to loosen the grip of the introjects of those figures and exposes the past to current realities" (p. 153). Williamson (1982a) suggested that the direct meeting of the parents and the adult client is the sine qua non of the therapy venture.

In contrast, Bowen (1978) did not require the presence of the parents in therapy. Indeed, Bowen preferred to conduct marital therapy with the primary couple alone in order to create a natural triangle. This triangle provided a context for him to facilitate the family-of-origin detriangulation process. Bowen involved the parents indirectly, however, by sending his clients "home" in an effort to help them detriangulate from their families of origin.

Boszormenyi-Nagy and Ulrich (1981) appeared to stand somewhere in the middle of this issue. They did not require the parents/grandparents to attend therapy sessions, but they encouraged attendance if it would optimize a rejunctive movement (toward relatedness) within the family. Boszormenyi- Nagy and Spark (1973) considered the inclusion of the parents/grandparents to be positive, because children are often the targets of negative transference between the parents and grandparents. Watching the two generations of adults work out their conflicts can free children from their parentified or scape- goated role and teach them to work out conflicts with their own parents.

LENGTH OF FAMILY-OF-ORIGIN THERAPY

Most family-of-origin therapists tend to have longer treatment regimens than do other family therapists. Nichols (1984) attributed much of the extended treatment period to the fact that therapists who practice family-of-origin therapy typically place the responsibility for change on the client. In addition, they tend to have broader goal aspirations (e.g., differentiation, reconnection of emotional cut-offs) than do therapists who follow many other symptom-focused family therapy approaches. Furthermore, because family-of-origin experiences are extremely powerful influences, they are unlikely to be overcome in a short period of time, even if the techniques are strategic in nature.

Framo (1975) noted that it may take a considerable amount of therapy time to prepare clients for a family-of-origin session. He, of course, distinguished sessions in which family-of-origin issues are discussed from sessions in which the parents are actually present in the therapy room. Because clients usually strongly resist the idea of including their parents in a therapy session, it may be necessary to treat people in a group for some time before they accept the idea.

According to Kramer (1985), family-of-origin therapy does not always have to be long-term. She noticed that, when the individual is unable to make decisions, the "decisional paralysis" may have its roots in the family of origin. She suggested that 4 to 12 sessions of family-of-origin therapy may overcome the impasse. Kramer is currently involved in obtaining more data on cases of "brief" family-of-origin therapy.

CONCLUSION

Professionals who use family-of-origin therapy, although they vary some-what in theory and technique, are concerned about the "baggage" that individuals carry around from their families of origin into their present relationships. They view this "baggage" as a potential obstacle to the establishment of solid marital and nuclear family relationships. They encourage clients to explore the past in order to readjust present relationships, basically viewing differentiation from and ties to the family of origin as the most optimal position. In essence, they want clients to make statements and behave in ways that are more clearly their own.

REFERENCES

Boszormenyi-Nagy, I., & Spark, G.M. (1973). *Invisible loyalties: Reciprocity in intergenerational family therapy*. New York: Harper & Row.

Boszormenyi-Nagy, I., & Ulrich, D.N. (1981). Contextual family therapy. In A.S. Gurman & D.P. Kniskern (Eds.), *Handbook of family therapy* (pp. 159–186). New York: Brunner/Mazel.

Bowen, M. (1978). *Family therapy in clinical practice*. New York: Jason Aronson.

Bray, J.H., & Williamson, D.S. (1987). Assessment of intergenerational family relationships. In A.E. Hovestadt & M. Fine (Eds.), *Family of origin therapy*. Rockville, MD: Aspen Publishers.

Fine, M. (1984). Minor point, major field? *Family Therapy News, 15*, 8.

Framo, J.L. (1975). Personal reflections of a family therapist. *Journal of Marriage and Family Counseling, 1*, 15–28.

Framo, J.L. (1981). The integration of marital therapy with sessions with the family of origin. In A.S. Gurman & D.P. Kniskern (Eds.), *Handbook of family therapy* (pp. 131–158). New York: Brunner/Mazel.

Guldner, C. A. (1987). Family-of-origin therapy within sex therapy. In A.J. Hovestadt and M. Fine (Eds.), *Family-of-origin therapy* (pp. 57–67). Rockville, MD: Aspen Publishers.

Gurman, A.S. (1984). The name game. *Family Therapy News, 15*, 8.

Headley, L. (1977). *Adults and their parents in family therapy: A new direction in treatment*. New York: Plenum Press.

Keeney, B.P. (1983). *Aesthetics of change*. New York: Guilford Press.

Kramer, J.R. (1985). *Family interfaces: Transgenerational patterns*. New York: Brunner/Mazel.

McGoldrick, M., & Gerson, R. (1985). *Genograms in family assessment*. New York: W.W. Norton.

Nadelson, C.C., & Paolino, M.D., Jr. (1978). Marital therapy from a psychoanalytic perspective. In T.J. Paolino, Jr., & B.S. McCrady (Eds.), *Marriage and marital therapy: Psychoanalytic, behavioral, and systems perspectives* (pp. 89–164). New York: Brunner/Mazel.

Nichols, M. (1984). *Family therapy: Concepts and methods*. New York: Gardner Press.

Pressman, B. (1987). The place of family-of-origin therapy in the treatment of wife abuse. In A.E. Hovestadt & M. Fine (Eds.), *Family of origin therapy*. Rockville, MD: Aspen Publishers.

Segraves, T.R. (1982). *Marital therapy: A combined psychodynamic-behavioral approach*. New York: Plenum Medical Book Co.

Williamson, D.S. (1978). New life at the graveyard: A method of therapy for individuation from a dead former parent. *Journal of Marital and Family Therapy, 4*, 93–101.

Williamson, D.S. (1981). Personal authority via termination of intergenerational hierarchical boundary: A "new" stage in the family life cycle. *Journal of Marital and Family Therapy, 7*, 441–452.

Williamson, D.S. (1982a). Personal authority via termination of the intergenerational hierarchical boundary: Part II. The consultation process and the therapeutic method. *Journal of Marital and Family Therapy, 8*, 23–37.

Williamson, D.S. (1982b). Personal authority in family experience via termination of the intergenerational hierarchical boundary: Part III. Personal authority defined, and the power of play in the change process. *Journal of Marital and Family Therapy, 8*, 309–323.

3. Intergenerational Participation in the Family Therapy Process

James Gladstone, PhD
Baycrest Centre for Geriatric Care
Toronto, Ontario

Many family therapists work only with the nuclear family. Extended family members may be exluded from therapy, either because their input is considered irrelevant, or because they are regarded as negative influences interfering with the effective functioning of the nuclear family. Efforts are often made to tighten intergenerational boundaries and encourage the autonomy of the nuclear family without acknowledging bonds of affection and commitment. This approach, however, views the nuclear family as a closed system. Intergenerational participation can enhance the therapy process and is consistent with a conceptualization of the family as an open system. Specific issues that are addressed include: (1) therapeutic goals; (2) whom to involve in therapy; and (3) factors associated with a positive therapeutic outcome.

THERAPEUTIC GOALS

Several reasons have been cited for including parents in clinical work with adult children. Framo (1976b, 1981) noted the importance of resolving intergenerational conflict and establishing adult-to-adult relationships between parents and their adult children. Parents can be encouraged to discuss previously guarded subjects, which helps adult children to learn more about themselves and gain a stronger sense of individual or family identity. On the other hand, parents can be discouraged from interfering in the lives of their adult children so that the younger generation can have more privacy and establish more control over their own lives.

Similarly, Williamson (1978) refers to the value of more peerlike relationships between adult children and their parents. Bowen (1978) emphasized that continual contacts of adult children with their parents facilitate the process of differentiation. Spark (1974, 1977), as well as Boszormenyi-Nagy and Spark (1973), described the "invisible loyalties" that adult children feel toward their parents. Adult children must rebalance their time, their energy, and the sense of obligation that they feel to their parents in order to improve the quality of their marriages. Spark and Brody (1970) and Framo (1976a) stated that the participation of the parents in sessions with adult children can open up areas of communication, challenge family myths, and prevent the repetition of dysfunctional patterns in future generations.

> Larry F., aged 41, had been divorced from his wife for 3 years. Fearing that he would lose contact with his two children, who were living with their mother, Larry began to telephone their home daily. This led to renewed conflict between Larry and his former spouse, who threatened to deny Larry access to the children. Larry contacted a therapist.
>
> During the first interview, the therapist noted that Larry's telephone calls to his children increased around the time that his 66-year-old father suffered a heart attack. Therefore, the therapist arranged a meeting with Larry and his father. At this meeting, Larry expressed his fear of being left alone when his father passed away. Mr. F., whom Larry had described as "the strong pillar who holds up the family," told Larry how much he had admired the way in which Larry coped with the stress surrounding his divorce. Furthermore, Mr. F. spoke about his own self-perceived failings as a father and his wish that he had been as good a father to Larry as he thought Larry was being to his own two children. Larry, who had never heard his father talk about his emotions so openly, left the session feeling somewhat unsettled.
>
> The therapist held two more sessions with Larry and his parents. Mr. F. continued to validate Larry as a person and said that he wished he had spent more time with Larry in previous years. The new closeness that seemed to develop between Larry and his father coincided with a reduction in Larry's telephone calls to his own children.

Therapists generally formulate the goals of intergenerational therapy with adult children in mind. Relatively few therapists consider the advantages of intergenerational therapy for the parents of adult children. In other words, when intergenerational family members are drawn upon in therapy, it is usually the older parent who is given the opportunity to help his or her child. Adult children are much less likely to be called upon when original contact is made with older parents. Yet our doing so may have very positive results for older clients. Opening up new channels for parent-child communication, resolving longstanding conflict, developing an adult-to-adult relationship, and rebalancing "invisible loyalties" are all interactive processes; as such, they are issues not only for adult children, but also for older parents.

> Mr. M., a 62-year-old man who had been a widower for 4 years, was planning to remarry. He was concerned that his two adult daughters, both of whom had been very close to their mother, would not accept his new wife. Mr. M. sought help from a therapist, who arranged a family session so that Mr. M. and his daughters could discuss their feelings about the impending marriage. Mr M.'s oldest daughter accused her father's fiancée of being interested only in her father's money. Mr. M. rebuked his daughter and added that he was "old enough to leave home" without asking for his daughter's advice. The therapist gently asked about Mr. M.'s first wife. After a few moments of silence, Mr. M. slowly started to talk about his first wife and how much he missed her. Mr. M.'s daughters said that they had never been able to discuss their mother's death with their father and had begun to interpret his plans to remarry as a "sign of disloyalty" to their mother.

The idea that intergenerational participation in family therapy can help both the older parent generation and their adult children can be taken even further. If the family is conceptualized as a social system, family therapists who conduct intergenerational counseling should not only consider the well-being of one generation or another, but also should provide services to the whole *system*.

> Mrs. L., aged 53, was concerned about the welfare of her 6-year-old granddaughter, Janet, who had lived with her since birth. Mrs. L.'s 24-year-old daughter, Kelly, had never married Janet's father and had had no contact with him since Janet was born. Although Mrs. L. and Kelly had "always had a rather stormy relationship," Kelly had left her newborn infant with her mother and moved across the country "so that she could find herself." Mrs. L. contacted a family therapist because Kelly had recently

returned, was married and pregnant, and wanted Janet to live with her and her new husband.

The therapist met first with Mrs. L. and then with Mrs. L. and Janet. Each expressed deep caring for the other. The therapist then arranged a meeting with Mrs. L., her daughter, and her son-in-law. Mrs. L. and Kelly referred to their past difficulties in communication and spoke about their desire to get to know each other as adults. Mother and daughter talked about their expectations of one another as a parent, a child, and a grandparent. The therapist pointed out that Mrs. L. and Kelly needed each other's support in caring for Janet, who, in turn, would benefit from having available to her both a mother and a grandmother. Kelly's new husband expressed his eagerness and his fears about becoming a father, as well as a husband and a member of a new extended family.

In subsequent sessions, the therapist continued to stress the need for each family member to allow the others time to adjust to their new roles. The family agreed not to remove Janet from Mrs. L.'s home, but to have Janet visit Kelly and her new husband regularly and to extend the duration of each visit over time.

By providing opportunities for family members to improve or consolidate relationships across generations, therapists recognize the openness of the intergenerational family system. A primary goal for therapy should be to assess the way that information permeates several intergenerational boundaries. This process is related to the way in which messages are received, interpreted, and transmitted by family members, as well as the extent to which development can occur in the system.

FAMILY MEMBERS TO BE INVOLVED IN THERAPY

Family members are invited to participate in therapy primarily on the basis of their perceived contribution to a client's difficulty or their perceived potential ability to eliminate the difficulty or reduce its severity. While older parents may be included most often in intergenerational counseling sessions, adult siblings may also be involved.

Several practitioners have noted the special importance that siblings may have in each other's lives. Bonds of loyalty and commitment between adult siblings may be qualitatively different, yet just as strong as those between parents and their adult children (Bank & Kahn, 1975; Headley, 1977; Framo, 1981). Although relationships with more genealogically removed members of the family are usually not as emotionally intense as those with members of the immediate family (Adams, 1968), uncles, aunts, and cousins may be actively involved with clients and provide valuable support (Leichter & Mitchell, 1978).

> Sally H., recently widowed at the age of 22, was trying to raise her 3-year-old son and 4-month-old daughter. Unemployed, Sally was receiving social assistance. She lived with her children in a small, one-bedroom apartment and had few friends or confidantes. As the stress in her life intensified, Sally found herself increasingly short-tempered with her son, whose behavior was becoming more aggressive. After striking her son in a rage, she called the Children's Aid Society and requested that her son be placed in a foster home.
>
> In the course of the assessment, the social worker investigated the possibility of placing Sally's son with a relative. Sally reported that she had "not been on speaking terms" with her parents for years and was close only to a sister, who was 8 years her senior. When the social worker contacted her, the sister agreed to take her nephew into her home temporarily. The social worker then arranged for someone to care for Sally's daughter a couple of times each week to allow Sally time for herself. In addition, Sally was given a special allowance for nutritional supplements and was referred to a family service agency for therapy. Sally then began to examine her role as a mother, her sense of isolation, and alternate ways that she could relate to her son when he returned to the apartment.

Family members need not be physically present in therapy sessions to participate in intergenerational counseling. After being "coached" by the therapist, individual clients may return to their families of origin and redefine their relationships with them (Bowen, 1978). The therapist may even help clients to "meet" symbolically with deceased family members whose memory has a powerful influence over their feelings, attitudes, and behaviors and to differentiate themselves emotionally from these family members (Paul & Paul, 1975; Williamson, 1978). Sometimes, the involvement of absent family members in an emotional sense is crucial for a client's efforts at individuation.

> Harriet P., aged 21, was afraid to leave the house to go to work for fear of being poisoned by all the pollutants in the air. When Harriet's fear generalized to the point that she was afraid to use detergents or disinfectants, she contacted a therapist.

At their first meeting, the therapist established that the onset of Harriet's symptoms coincided with the breakdown of her parents' marriage. Harriet indicated that nobody in the family discussed this event. Inquiring about other possible losses, the therapist learned that Harriet's older brother, Sol, whose emotional state had been diagnosed as "schizophrenic," had taken his own life 6 years earlier. Harriet, who had felt very close to Sol, had little information about her brother's condition or death, because the family did not discuss these subjects either.

With the therapist's support, Harriet met her father for dinner and expressed her concern for him. She told her father that she was worried about the effect that the breakdown of his marriage would have on him, as well as on her mother. Mr. P. replied that, whatever happened, he did not want to "lose" his daughter. Harriet then began to ask her father about Sol. Over the next few weeks, Mr. P. talked more about his son. Eventually, Harriet and her father visited the cemetery where Sol was buried. By this time, Harriet's symptoms had disappeared. A critical experience for Harriet was a "visit" to Sol that she made alone. She stood in front of his grave, wearing her blue jeans rather than the outfit that she reserved for formal occasions. As Harriet later reported to the therapist, this represented a "personal emancipation and the end of my mourning for my family."

Family members maintain different types of role relationships simultaneously, performing what Merton (1968) referred to as "multiple roles." For example, a senior member of the family may occupy the positions of parent, parent-in-law, and grandparent simultaneously. Thus, in considering the nature of family members' involvement in therapy, the therapist must determine not only *who* should participate in counseling, but on the basis of *which role* or roles should that person be asked to participate.

Irene J., aged 36, was recently divorced from her husband of 14 years. Irene retained custody of her three children. Feeling lonely and depressed, she worried about raising her children as a single parent. She was on good terms with her parents, and they had provided her with emotional and material support immediately after her separation from her husband. In fact, Irene was concerned about growing too dependent on her parents, which further undermined her already shaken perception of herself as a strong and self-reliant individual.

In asking Irene to bring her parents to a session, the therapist emphasized that they were not being invited as parents, but as grandparents. During that session, the therapist complimented Irene's parents for their ability to help their daughter at the time of the separation and complimented Irene for her own ability to cope under stress. The therapist added that the purpose of their meeting was to determine how Irene's parents could continue to enjoy their relationships with their grandchildren and provide support to the youngsters after the breakdown of their daughter's marriage. The grandparents offered to pay half of their daughter's mortgage, and Irene's mother volunteered to help her daughter prepare meals for the grandchildren. While this assistance would benefit Irene, it was directed primarily to the welfare of the grandchildren; the grandparents did not want their granchildren, whose home life had already been disrupted, to lose their home, and they were concerned about the grandchildren's nutrition. Irene did not feel that her parents were usurping her role as mother and agreed to this arrangement. As an indirect result, the arrangement relieved some of the pressures that Irene was feeling as a single parent.

The specific family members involved in counseling are determined partly by the therapist's working definition of *family*. If the family is perceived as essentially nuclear in structure, the boundaries around the family system enclose primarily two generations. Clinical efforts are more likely to focus on parents and their children, who are considered to take part in mutually reinforcing behaviors. If the definition of family is expanded both horizontally and vertically, however, a host of new intergenerational relationships become readily apparent. This altered perception suggests that family members across the generations have a potential or actual impact on the clinical issue. Moreover, for both the individual client and the practitioner, intergenerational participation in the therapy process can assume a new and more productive meaning.

FACTORS ASSOCIATED WITH A POSITIVE THERAPEUTIC OUTCOME

Several practitioners have proposed models for working with the family of origin and the larger intergenerational family. When conducting family-of-origin work, Framo (1976b, 1981) and Headley (1977) arranged sessions for individual clients and their parents or siblings. The clients' spouses are generally excluded from the sessions in order to prevent triangulation, but they are given the opportunity to listen to the session on audiotape. Boszormenyi-Nagy and Spark (1973) and Spark (1974, 1977) are more flexible in terms of whom they invite to a session, placing an individual who is not considered to be directly involved in the issue at hand as an "observer." Bowen (1978) usually meets with his individual clients alone, but encourages them to plan a series of visits with their family of origin so that they can gradually reach a higher level of individuation. Bank and Kahn (1975), as well as Headley (1977), suggest a format for meeting with siblings; Williamson (1978) proposes ways to coach clients who are trying to resolve issues with a deceased family member; and Kuypers and Trute (1978) address some important issues related to work with older families, such as the struggle that each generation may have with its own aging process. Hartman (1979) pointed out the value of formulating hypotheses as a guide for clinical intervention.

Many of these paractitioners have stated that therapists should adopt a directive style in intergenerational family sessions. An intense emotional climate often accompanies these meetings, and therapists should try to prevent blaming, long outbursts of anger, and defensive posturing on the part of family members. At the same time, therapists should offer support, compliment the efforts of family members to resolve difficulties, and focus on positive aspects of their relationships.

A number of other factors may be associated with a therapist's success with intergenerational therapy. For example, therapists should be sensitive to the ethnic background of their clients. Some ethnic groups promote close-knit ties, while others place a greater value on independence and self-sufficiency (McGoldrick, Pearce, & Giordano, 1982). Clients' willingness to accept intergenerational involvement may depend on their cultural values regarding self-determination.

Framo (1976b, 1981) and Headley (1977) generally delay asking their clients to bring older parents to a session until they have established clear working contracts with their clients. Therapists should present specific reasons for including relatives in therapy sessions. Moreover, these reasons must make sense to the clients. Therapists should also have developed a trusting relationship with their clients before undertaking intergenerational therapy. Although therapists cannot give guarantees, they can give hope that meeting with older parents, siblings, or other family members can make a positive difference in their clients' lives.

If there is no clear working contract, if clients are unsure of the therapist's commitment to helping them, or if clients do not believe that meetings with their parents may be helpful, intergenerational therapy is less likely to be an effective part of the therapy process.

Mr. and Mrs. S. went to a therapist for marital counseling. It became increasingly clear to both the therapist and the couple that many of the marital problems stemmed from their individual relationships with their respective families of origin. The therapist was new to the case, however, and had not established a trusting relationship with the couple. Furthermore, the therapist insisted that Mr. and Mrs. S. bring their parents to a therapy session so early in the therapy process that the couple found the idea extremely threatening. As the therapist did not offer the couple any other mode of therapy, they terminated their involvement with this therapist and sought another.

CONCLUSION

As life expectancy continues to increase, family therapists will be working with more and more clients who are members of three- and even four-generation families. Moreover, as the post–World War II "baby boom" generation ages, there will be a growing number of clients whose problems involve relationships with family members in both ascending and descending generations. This phenomenon will present family therapists with additional challenges. When family therapists encourage intergenerational participation in the therapy process, they provide the family with an opportunity to act as a mutual aid group. Furthermore, they facilitate their own roles as change agents by surrounding themselves with human resources who can help them initiate change and engender growth in the family system.

REFERENCES

Adams, B.N. (1968). *Kinship in an urban setting*. Chicago: Markham.

Bank, S., & Kahn, M.D. (1975). Sisterhood-brotherhood is powerful: Sibling sub-systems and family therapy. *Family Process, 14*, 311–337.

Boszormenyi-Nagy, I., & Spark, G.M. (1973). *Invisible loyalties. Reciprocity in intergenerational family therapy*. New York: Harper & Row.

Bowen, M. (1978). *Family therapy in clinical practice*. New York: Jason Aronson.

Framo, J.L. (1976a). Chronicle of a struggle to establish a family unit within a community mental health center. In P.J. Guerin, Jr. (Ed.), *Family therapy: Theory and practice* (pp. 23–39). New York: Gardner Press.

Framo, J.L. (1976b). Family of origin as a therapeutic resource for adults in marital and family therapy: You can and should go home again. *Family Process, 15*, 193–210.

Framo, J.L. (1981). The integration of marital therapy with sessions with family of origin. In A.S. Gurman & D.P. Kniskern (Eds.), *Handbook of family therapy* (pp. 133–158). New York: Brunner/Mazel.

Hartman, L.A. (1979). The extended family as a resource for change: An ecological approach to family-centered practice. In C.B. Germain (Ed.), *Social work practice: People and environments. An ecological perspective* (pp. 239–266). New York: Columbia University Press.

Headley, L. (1977). *Adults and their parents in family therapy*. New York: Plenum Press.

Kuypers, J.A., & Trute, B. (1978). The older family as the locus of crisis intervention. *The Family Coordinator, 27*, 405–411.

Leichter, H.J., & Mitchell, W.E. (1978). *Kinship and casework*. New York: Teachers College Press, Columbia University.

McGoldrick, M., Pearce, J.K., & Giordano, J. (1982). *Ethnicity and family therapy*. New York: Guilford Press.

Merton, R.K. (1968). *Social theory and social structure*. New York: The Free Press.

Paul, N.L., & Paul, B.B. (1975). *A marital puzzle*. New York: W.W. Norton.

Spark, G.M. (1974). Grandparents and intergenerational family therapy. *Family Process, 13*, 225–237.

Spark, G.M. (1977). Marriage is a family affair. *The Family Coordinator, 26*, 167–174.

Spark, G.M., & Brody, E.M. (1970). The aged are family members. *Family Process, 7*, 195–210.

Williamson, D.S. (1978). New life at the graveyard: A method of therapy for individuation from a dead former parent. *Journal of Marriage and Family Counseling, 4*, 93–101.

4. Assessment of Intergenerational Family Relationships

James H. Bray, PhD
Associate Professor
Department of Psychology
Texas Woman's University
Houston, Texas

Donald S. Williamson, PhD
Director
Houston Family Institute
Houston, Texas

Several theoretical and therapeutic systems within the multigenerational, intergenerational, or transgenerational perspectives share common bases for understanding families across several generations of family evolution (Boszormenyi-Nagy & Spark, 1973; Bowen, 1978; Framo, 1981; Paul, 1981; Williamson, 1981). The intergenerational perspective is a synthesis and extension of previous multigenerational models that have been developed by Williamson, Bray, and others (Bray, Harvey, & Williamson, 1986; Bray, Williamson, & Malone, 1984a; Harvey & Bray, 1985; Williamson, 1981, 1982a, 1982b; Williamson & Bray, 1985).

From this perspective, it is assumed that relational patterns are learned and passed down across the generations and that current individual and family behavior is a result of these patterns. Thus, accurate assessment of relational patterns, both functional and dysfunctional, not only is the first step in understanding families from an intergenerational perspective, but also is an essential step for proper treatment.

Several multigenerational family theorists state that it is necessary to assess patterns across 3 to 10 generations in order to understand family functioning completely. The intergenerational point of view focuses somewhat narrowly on two generations, namely, adults in the third to fifth decades of life and their older parents. In other words, the political and relational patterns that exist between the adult and the older parents are the focus of attention, the behaviors that must be changed, and, consequently, the points of intervention.

KEY CONCEPTS OF THE INTERGENERATIONAL PERSPECTIVE

Two distinct processes influence family functioning: multigenerational family patterning and family life cycle development (Williamson & Bray, 1986). Family development and individual development are the basic building blocks of a multigenerational theoretical perspective. The ongoing process of development across the generations and the ways in which various interactional and emotional patterns are learned or transmitted across generations are major foci of this approach.

Multigenerational Family Patterning

Family theorists have developed several key concepts to describe family relationships, family process, and the development and transmission of interactional patterns across generations. Relational patterns result from a combination of overt and covert expectations and attributions of family members. These expectations and attributions are translated into behavior patterns through the reinforcement of specific behaviors and through social learning and modeling (Bandura, 1977; Williamson & Bray, 1986). Differentiation of self, triangulation, covert loyalties, unresolved grief reactions, intimacy, and personal authority are key family patterns to assess in intergenerational family relationships.

Differentiation of self, or individuation, involves two processes: one within individuals and one in their relationships with others (Bowen, 1978; Kerr, 1981, 1984). Within an individual, differentiation is the degree to which the individual is able to discriminate between thoughts and emotions, controls his or her own thoughts and feelings, considers his or her own judgment an adequate basis for action, and takes full responsibility for the consequences of these actions. In relationships, differentiation is the degree to which an individual operates in an autonomous manner. A differentiated person is able to function optimally around important others without feeling responsible for them, controlled by them, or impaired by them. A differentiated family can allow its members to function independently and autonomously, even in the face of stress and anxiety. Differentiated families promote the health and growth of each member in a manner that is not at the expense of other family members.

Fusion is the opposite pole from differentiation of self. Fusion refers to how emotionally "stuck together" persons are in relationships. People who have a high level of fusion do not have a clear sense of self as individuals; function in a dependent, emotionally reflexive, semiautomatic, or irrational manner in relationships; and are more likely to develop symptoms in the face of stress. The level of fusion reflects the degree of unresolved emotional attachment to the family of origin. In families, fusion is indicated by family members' attempts to think for each other, feel for each other, and/or function for each other. When the level of family fusion is high, one or more family members usually develop some impairment or symptom.

Some individuals emotionally cut off contact with the family of origin as a means of dealing with fusion. They may express this emotional cut-off by limiting their physical contact with the family of origin, such as by making only obligatory holiday visits or infrequent telephone calls, or by distancing themselves psychologically, such as by withdrawing into books, fantasy, or by being preoccupied with health concerns (Kerr, 1981, 1984). Initially, these individuals may appear to be differentiated, but individuals who emotionally cut themselves off from their family of origin experience the same kinds of problems that undifferentiated individuals experience. These people also have a tendency to overinvest in current relationships, which puts added pressure on them to succeed in their relationships.

It is assumed that the basic level of differentiation or fusion in a family is reflected by individual family members and vice versa. Thus, if one family member appears very differentiated, but other family members are symptomatic, the basic level of differentiation of each person is assumed to be the average of all family members' levels of differentiation.

Bowen (1978) proposed that the two-person system, or dyad, is inherently unstable because of the inevitable fusion between individuals in relationships. People decrease the anxiety or stress in the dyad by triangulating a third person. There is a certain amount of tension in any triangled relationship, however, because invariably two parties are "in" and the third is "out." In most triangulated relationships, this process is constantly changing. When the interactions between the three people get stuck, the triangle frequently becomes pathological. Because triangles are formed in response to stress and fusion, they may be observable and changeable only when there is sufficient stress and anxiety in the family system (Bowen, 1978).

Loyalty and fairness to the family of origin are basic premises in relational behavior. Covert or invisible loyalties that develop across generations strongly influence family relationship patterns (Boszormenyi-Nagy & Spark, 1973). Loyalty implies a certain amount of trust and commitment to a relationship. Invisible loyalties are mandates that operate at an unconscious or "underground" level to mold and direct individual behavior. For example, adult children may create problems in their marriages out of loyalty to their parents, who have or had a troubled marriage. It would be especially embarrassing for the parental marriage if their children's marriages were significantly better, thus making theirs look even worse by comparison. Such an expression of loyalty reflects an attempt to repay some indebtedness to the family of origin;

however, because it operates in a covert manner, it is likely to produce dysfunction in families.

A related concept is that of split loyalties. This occurs when an individual involved in a conflicted relationship triangle can only be loyal to one person at the expense of loyalty to the other. The most common example of this occurs when a child (of any age) has a split in loyalty to the parents.

Paul (1981) hypothesized that, if one generation experiences a significant loss and does not mourn it, the unexpressed grief is passed to subsequent generations. This is likely to result in individual and relational dysfunction in the new generation, as illustrated in *A Marital Puzzle* (Paul & Paul, 1975). Severe medical illnesses or tragedies in earlier generations may have a similar effect. All these events must be assessed for their potential effects on family functioning.

Intimacy is defined as the ability to be close to another person while maintaining clear boundaries of identity (Lewis, Beavers, Gossett, & Phillips, 1976; Williamson, 1982b). It is composed of four parts: (1) trust, (2) love–fondness, (3) self-disclosure, and (4) commitment (Bray, Williamson, & Malone, 1984a). A type of "voluntary fusion," intimacy can be initiated or terminated at the discretion of the individual. The voluntariness and boundaries distinguish the closeness of intimacy from that of fusion.

As described by Williamson (1981, 1982b), personal authority in the family system (PAFS) is associated with a life cycle stage that occurs when adults are between 30 and 45 years old. In this stage, individuals resolve the inherent tension between differentiation and intimacy in the biological family and in other significant personal relationships. PAFS has three primary characteristics (Williamson, 1982b):

1. the ability to order and direct one's own thoughts and feelings, to choose to express or not to express these thoughts and feelings, to respect one's judgments as an adequate basis for action, and to take full responsibility for the consequences of these actions (i.e., differentiation as described earlier)
2. the ability to initiate, receive, or decline to receive intimacy, voluntarily, and to tolerate the same freedom in significant others, while simultaneously maintaining clear self boundaries
3. the ability to relate to all other human beings, including one's parents, as peers in the fundamental experience of being human. While most people focus on these issues in their fourth and fifth decades of life, the precursors of PAFS are relevant for all individuals.

PAFS is a continuum with personal authority at one pole and intergenerational intimidation at the other. Personal authority is reflected in the behavioral patterns that are characteristic of an integrated and differentiated self (Bowen, 1978), such as the exercise of choice over individual destiny in life and the pursuit of personal health and well-being. A person with such personal authority can remain connected and intimate with the family of origin, while simultaneously acting from a differentiated position *within* the family of origin (Bray, Williamson, & Malone, 1984a; Williamson, 1981, 1982b).

Family Life Cycle Development

Predictable and unpredictable changes and events occur throughout the family life cycle (Carter & McGoldrick, 1980). The predictable family life cycle events reflect common stages and sequences that families encounter through time. It is hypothesized that the transition from one stage to the next can be stressful for families, because it requires changes in family relationships and the development of new coping skills and behaviors. The unpredictable events that occur in the family life cycle are usually beyond the family's control, such as wars, economic recessions, or unexpected deaths. Although somewhat discrete stages or time periods have been identified, most families progress through them in their own unique fashion.

Problem Development

Fusion occurs and unresolved emotional issues resurface when a certain level of stress and anxiety develops in a family; this level is unique for each family. Often, problems and symptoms appear at this time. The stresses come from interactions between family members, external life stresses, and family life cycle changes. Because transitions between family life cycle stages can be particularly stressful, symptoms are more likely to develop during transitions.

Bowen (1978) stated that symptoms are usually expressed in three ways:

1. marital conflict
2. dysfunction in a spouse, involving physical illness, psychological dysfunction, and/or social dysfunction
3. similar dysfunction in one or more children as a result of triangulation.

One or all of these types of problems may develop in a family over time. The symptoms are simply expressions of the way in which a family responds to stress, given its basic level of differentiation and types of covert loyalties. The higher the level of differentiation, the greater the stress that the family can withstand before symptoms develop. In addition, a more differentiated family "bounces back" more quickly from a stressful event than does a less differentiated family.

METHODS OF ASSESSMENT

Assessment of clients is an ongoing procedure during the therapy process. The assessment includes not only current psychological and social functioning, but also physical health status (Williamson & Bray, 1985). Such an assessment is essential for a complete understanding of family functioning. Several methods for evaluating intergenerational relationships are discussed in the literature. Two of the foremost are the clinical interview and the client self-report on the *Personal Authority in the Family System Questionnaire* (Bray, Williamson, & Malone, 1984a, 1984b).

The Clinical Interview

The first step in assessing family-of-origin relationships is the clinical interview. While this interview focuses on the current problem and other areas of functioning, the clinician tries also to understand the problem in a three-generation family context. At first, clients do not usually understand the relevance of such a context to their problems and symptoms, and the clinician must establish the context by asking the right kinds of questions and "seeding" the interview with suggestions or statements about intergenerational family relationships.

Initially, the clinician takes a family history that focuses on family relationships and patterns of development over time. The clinician then adopts a multigenerational focus by inquiring into relational patterns across the generations. Unresolved issues, covert loyalties, and health problems receive special attention. The clinician may use a genogram to summarize the client's family relationships (Guerin & Pendagast, 1976). A list of important life events on the genogram (e.g., divorces, significant illnesses) and life changes (e.g., moves, new jobs) provides a concise social and psychological record of the client and family.

Some clinicians ask the client to write a history of growing up in his or her family of origin (Williamson, 1982a) and to read the history aloud during the session. When the client reads the history aloud, the clinician can evaluate the nonverbal signs and the emotionality associated with the history. The clinician may also ask the client to go back over the history and, using an imaginary yellow marker, highlight the key memories, incidents, and attitudes that continue to stand out sharply in the client's present emotionality. This identifies and delineates the continuing unresolved issues in the intergenerational process so that the clinician can explore them further in order to determine their complexity and intensity as they continue to survive and flourish at the different levels of the client's consciousness.

When the client omits from the history important areas in the developmental sequence of his or her life, the clinician may ask about them as a matter of simple curiosity or to "see what gives." Hypotheses about these areas may come from what is "unsaid" through nonverbal cues. This is a process not unlike "testing the limits" in the review with a client of his/her responses to the Rorschach Ink Blots. That which is forgotten or denied is often as useful in identifying the necessary agenda for intergenerational work as is that which is freely discussed. In this sense, writing and reviewing the autobiography is like offering an ambiguous stimulus so that the client provides externally unstructured and, therefore, highly internally structured responses.

When gathering the family history and constructing the genogram, it is important to assess the current life cycle stage for both the individual and the family. Attention to life cycle changes further clarifies the context of the problems and may have important implications for treatment. Thus, it is important to evaluate (1) the problems and symptoms associated with the current stage, (2) the ways in which the family has coped with previous life cycle transitions, and (3) the ways in which the client's family of origin coped with similar life cycle stages. The interview should focus on major illnesses, deaths, and other potentially unresolved issues.

Observing how the client describes the family, rather than focusing only on the content of the interview, also provides important data. The clinician can assess the level of differentiation, fusion, or personal authority by listening to the client's descriptions. Less differentiated individuals tend to blame others for their actions (e.g., "I did it because she made me do it."), do not take responsibility for their own lives and health, and/or are frequently indecisive. The use of "we statements" (e.g., "In our family, we have this problem.") when referring to a specific individual in the family reflects a high level of fusion in the family. A person who is intimidated by significant hierarchical figures, especially the parents, has little personal authority and often responds to the intimidation with fear, disappointment, anger, or rage at the parental figures. Such individuals are inhibited and generally function less effectively, particularly around authority figures, than do individuals with more personal authority. They also have difficulty forming close, intimate relationships and may function poorly in their work or profession (Bray, Williamson, & Malone, 1986). Problems with relationships and work often reflect covert loyalties to the family of origin.

More differentiated individuals express their opinions through "I statements," such as, "I think, I believe, I want, I prefer," rather than "we statements." Individuals behaving with personal authority also take responsibility and make decisions for their lives and are not intimidated by authority figures. Differentiation and a high level of personal authority are reflected in better overall physical health and a healthy life style. Although the nonmedical psychotherapist often overlooks this correlation, it is very important for evaluating individual and family functioning. The clinician may gather health information by means of an intake form and follow-up questions about the responses. Information about hospitalizations, visits to physicians, physicians' reports and recommendations, as well as present and previous use of medications should be gathered. The inquiry should include information about the client's diet, exercise, general patterns of stress (both physical and emotional), and usual ways of coping with stress. Of particular concern are the client's own sense of physical well-being and the client's intentions, explanations, and fears for both the short-term and the long-term future.

Further inquiry about transgenerational patterns of physical "dis-ease" and an exploration of the present generation's fears also should be covered. It is important to understand the client's perceptions of events, rather than finding out the "truth" about what "really happened" in the family of origin, because the ongoing internal perceptions are the points of intervention. In addition, the clinician should be attentive to and gently draw the client's attention to aspects of the client's physical presence that suggest concern. This includes a heavy physical presence, both literally and metaphorically, as shown by such signs as heavy sighing, difficulty in breathing, teary or sad eyes, dizziness, or numbness in the arms or legs after sitting. The clinician may ask, for example, about the wellness of the client's heart, at all levels; about what cannot be stomached or easily swallowed; who is a pain in the neck or butt; who or what is breaking one's back; or when the client feels like throwing up, etc. In short, the clinician encourages an open dialogue, however symbolic, between the client's body and the client's "inner self" so that the client cannot absorb family emotionality physically without some degree of awareness and, therefore, a possibility for renegotiation and open expression. In this way, the client learns to relate patterns of physical stress and dis-ease to patterns of conflict and loss of self in the larger intergenerational family experience.

Personal Authority in the Family System

Bray, Williamson, and Malone (1984a, 1984b) designed a self-report instrument, the *Personal Authority in the Family System Questionnaire (PAFS-Q)*, to assess intergenerational processes in the three-generation family system. Individuals rate their *current* relationships with members of their family of origin and members of their nuclear family or a person with whom they have an intimate dyadic relationship. There are three versions of the *PAFS-Q*. Version A is for adults with children, Version B is for adults without children, and Version C is for young adults and college-aged students without children.

Version A has eight nonoverlapping scales that provide a measure of the behaviors and processes discussed earlier:

1. The Spousal Fusion/Individuation Scale measures the degree to which a person operates in a fused or individuated manner with the spouse or significant other.
2. The Intergenerational Fusion/Individuation Scale measures the degree to which a person operates in a fused or individuated manner with parents.
3. The Spousal Intimacy Scale measures the degree of intimacy and satisfaction with the spouse or significant other.
4. The Intergenerational Intimacy Scale measures the degree of intimacy and satisfaction with parents. Items on this scale are answered separately for mother and father.
5. The Nuclear Family Triangulation Scale measures the triangulation of spouses and their children.
6. The Intergenerational Triangulation Scale measures the triangulation of a person and his or her parents.
7. The Intergenerational Intimidation Scale measures the degree of personal intimidation experienced by an individual relative to his or her parents.
8. The Personal Authority Scale measures the interactional aspects of personal authority as defined by Williamson (1982b).

Version B simply excludes the Nuclear Family Triangulation Scale. Version C also excludes the Nuclear Family Triangulation Scale and is modified for a college-aged population (Bray & Harvey, 1986). All three versions can be scored either by hand or by computer.

Larger scores on the intimacy, individuation, and personal authority scales signify higher levels of those characteristics. Larger scores on the triangulation and intimidation scales indicate lower levels of those characteristics. A highly differentiated person scores high on the intimacy, individuation, and personal authority scales, but low on the triangulation and intimidation scales. High scores on the intimacy and intimidation scales, combined with low scores on the individuation scales, reflect the classic pattern of fused or undifferentiated relationships. Often, people with such scores are happy or satisfied with the relationship, but develop symptoms as a result of their dependency or lack of autonomy. Conversely, people with low scores on the intimacy and individuation scales, or a low score on the intimacy scale and a high score on the intimidation scale, are indicating an emotional cut-off from the family of origin. It is useful to keep these profiles in mind when assessing family function. Currently, there are no cut off points to categorize people as differentiated or triangulated for the *PAFS-Q*; rather, an analysis of the profile using all the scores on the questionnaire is employed to assess the family system.

The *PAFS-Q* has multiple applications in the therapeutic process. As an assessment device to measure current family functioning, it may be administered when therapy begins or when family-of-origin issues become the focus of therapy. By comparing the scores of various family members, the clinician can note similarities and differences among various perceptions of family functioning. Sharing their responses on the *PAFS-Q* helps couples understand not only current nuclear family perceptions, but also the differences in family-of-origin relationships. The *PAFS-Q* given at different points in therapy can serve as a measure of change and self-evaluation. It is also useful as an intervention tool, because it requires clients to think about the current status of their intergenerational family relationships. Taking the *PAFS-Q* is not usually a neutral experience; it stimulates considerable thought about family-of-origin relationships.

> Mrs. K., aged 30, initially sought therapy because her 6-year-old son had been referred by school personnel for counseling. He was having behavior problems both at home and at school. Mr. K. came for one session, but refused to return for further sessions because it was "embarrassing and against his family upbringing" to seek help outside the family. It was "OK" for his wife and son to have therapy, but he would have nothing to do with it. Mrs. K. and her son underwent family therapy for the boy's behavior problems. Within three sessions, the boy's behavior began to improve.
>
> Because Mrs. K. appeared quite depressed and unhappy, therapy began to focus on her at this point. She reported that she was "very down," felt guilty about her "bad" parenting, and received considerable negative feedback from her mother about her ability to be a better parent. Although there were hints of marital problems, any attempt to focus on them met with considerable denial and resistance from Mrs. K. Further interviewing indicated considerable fusion with and intimidation by her parents. Her relationship with her father was somewhat distant, and she often had conflicts with her mother, particularly over Mrs. K.'s parenting.
>
> When the focus of therapy shifted to Mrs. K., she was asked to complete the *PAFS-Q* so that the therapist could assess her current family functioning and as an intervention to start her thinking about family of origin issues. As can be seen from Table 1, Mrs. K.'s *PAFS-Q* scores before therapy indicated below average individuation, personal authority, and triangulation. Although her intimidation score was not particularly low, she reported in the interviews considerable fear and anxiety about

Table 1 T Scores from the *PAFS-Q* Scales for Mrs. K.*

Scale	Before Therapy	During Therapy	After Therapy
Spousal Intimacy	49	56	47
Spousal Fusion/Individuation	40	36	46
Nuclear Family Triangulation	35	46	44
Intergenerational Intimacy	45	45	51
Intergenerational Fusion/Individuation	24	38	45
Intergenerational Triangulation	59	66	67
Intergenerational Intimidation	47	54	56
Personal Authority	27	39	51

*T scores have a mean of 50 and a standard deviation of 10. Scores greater than ± 1 standard deviation can be considered out of the normal range, with scores ± 2 standard deviations in the exceptional or pathological range.

discussing several subjects with her parents; this was reflected in her low personal authority score. Although Mrs. K. reported few problems with marital intimacy and satisfaction, she reported more spousal fusion. Taking the *PAFS-Q* introduced family-of-origin issues to Mrs. K., and she became quite interested in how these relationships might be affecting her current family. The therapist began working on these issues by following the general treatment plan outlined by Williamson (1982a).

After a couple of months in therapy, Mrs. K. again took the *PAFS-Q*. As can be seen from her scores, she reported some increase in individuation, personal authority, and considerable decrease in intimidation. The intimidation decreased after she was given specific assignments involving her parents. Mrs. K. did not ask her parents to participate in a therapy session, but worked on her own through visits to and from her parents. She reported after the second administration that taking the *PAFS-Q* "helped me realize some of the progress I have made and where I need to work further."

The final *PAFS-Q* scores indicated some additional increase in individuation and an additional decrease in intergenerational intimidation. When Mrs. K. left therapy, she still wanted to work on some things, but felt she could handle them by herself. Her initial symptoms of depression and unhappiness had lifted, and there were no longer any problems with her son. She felt much more comfortable with her parenting, less dependent on the approval of her parents and her husband, and better able to handle the stresses of family life. She had also suffered from regular and nagging illnesses, such as premenstrual syndrome, colds, and sinus infections, prior to therapy. After therapy, she noted that she had not had a cold in months and felt much healthier physically as well.

SUMMARY AND CONCLUSIONS

The accurate assessment of family relationships is an ongoing part of the therapeutic process throughout consultations with clients. Clinical assessments through interviewing, questioning, and observing the process of client interactions serve to identify what issues need to be focused on at any given point in the consultation process. While good basic clinical skills will provide the foundation for this, an intergenerational family focus is necessary to fully understand individual and family behavior from this perspective. By taking this point of view, many of the useful questions and areas of inquiry are readily apparent to the clinician. More formal assessment can be accomplished with instruments such as the *Personal Authority in the Family System Questionnaire.* In our experience this instrument serves a dual role as an evaluation of current family relationships and also as an intervention to help the client focus on intergenerational family issues. Future work will attempt to identify specific patterns of intergenerational dysfunction that can be assessed using the methods described in this article. This will in turn make interventions more successful.

REFERENCES

Bandura, A. (1977). *Social-learning theory.* Englewood Cliffs, NJ: Prentice-Hall.

Boszormenyi-Nagy, I., & Spark, G. (1973). *Invisible loyalties.* New York: Harper & Row.

Bowen, M. (1978). *Family therapy in clinical practice.* New York: Jason Aronson.

Bray, J.H., & Harvey, D.M. (1986). *Development of the college student version of the personal authority in the family system questionnaire.* Unpublished manuscript.

Bray, J.H., Harvey, D.M., & Williamson, D.S. (1986). *Intergenerational family relationships: An evaluation of theory and measurement. Psychotherapy* (in press).

Bray, J.H., Williamson, D.S., & Malone, P.E. (1984a). Personal authority in the family system: Development of a questionnaire to measure personal authority in intergenerational family processes. *Journal of Marital and Family Therapy, 10,* 167–178.

Bray, J.H., Williamson, D.S., & Malone, P.E. (1984b). *Personal authority in the family system questionnaire manual.* Houston Family Institute. Copies may be purchased from James H. Bray, Ph.D., Department of Psychology & Philosophy, Texas Woman's University, 1130 M.D. Anderson Blvd., Houston, TX 77030.

Bray, J.H., Williamson, D.S., & Malone, P.E. (1986). An evaluation of an intergenerational consultation process to increase personal authority in the family system. *Family Process, 25,* 423–436.

Carter, E.A., & McGoldrick, M. (Eds.). (1980). *The family life cycle: A framework for family therapy.* New York: Gardner Press.

Framo, J. (1981). The integration of marital therapy with sessions with family of origin. In A. Gurman & D. Kniskern (Eds.), *Handbook of family therapy* (pp. 133–158). New York: Brunner/Mazel.

Guerin, P.J., & Pendagast, E.G. (1976). Evaluation of a family system and genogram. In P.J. Guerin (Ed.), *Family therapy: Theory and practice* (pp. 450–464). New York: Gardner Press.

Harvey, D., & Bray, J.H. (1985). *Evaluation of an intergenerational theory of personal development: Family process determinants of psychological and health distress.* Unpublished manuscript.

Kerr, M.E. (1981). Family systems theory and therapy. In A. Gurman & D. Kniskern (Eds.), *Handbook of family therapy.* New York: Brunner/Mazel.

Kerr, M.E. (1984). Theoretical base for differentiation of self in one's family of origin. *The Clinical Supervisor, 2,* 3–36.

Lewis, J.M., Beavers, W.R., Gossett, J.T., & Phillips, V.A. (1976). *No single thread.* New York: Brunner/Mazel.

Paul, N. (1981). *The unconscious transmission of hidden images and the schizophrenic process.* Paper presented at the 7th International Symposium on the Psychotherapy of Schizophrenia, University of Heidelberg, West Germany, September 30–October 3.

Paul, N.L., & Paul, B.B. (1975). *A marital puzzle.* New York: W.W. Norton.

Williamson, D.S. (1981). Personal authority via termination of the intergenerational hierarchical boundary: A "new" stage in the family life cycle. *Journal of Marital and Family Therapy, 7,* 441–452.

Williamson, D.S. (1982a). Personal authority via termination of the intergenerational hierarchical boundary: Part II. The consultation process and the therapeutic method. *Journal of Marital and Family Therapy, 8,* 25–37.

Williamson, D.S. (1982b). Personal authority in family experience via termination of the intergenerational hierarchical boundary: Part III. Personal authority defined and the power of play in change-process. *Journal of Marital and Family Therapy, 8,* 309–323.

Williamson, D.S., & Bray, J.H. (1986). The intergenerational point of view. In S. Henoa & N. Gross (Eds.), *Family systems medicine* (pp. 90–110). New York: Brunner/Mazel.

Williamson, D.S., & Bray, J.H. (1987). Family development and change across the generations: An intergenerational point of view. In C.J. Falicov (Ed.), *Family transitions: Continuity and change over the life cycle.* New York: Guilford Press.

5. The Place of Family-of-Origin Therapy in the Treatment of Wife Abuse

Barbara Pressman, MEd
Wilfrid Laurier University
Faculty of Social Work
Waterloo, Ontario

The family-of-origin perspective plays a role in the treatment of wife abuse in three broad areas: (1) understanding the dynamics and the psychological basis of wife abuse, (2) diagnosis, and (3) the actual treatment both of the men who abuse women and of the women who are abused.

THE DYNAMICS OF WIFE ABUSE

In a well-functioning home (see Figure 1) described by Minuchin (1974), the functions of the parents are distinct and unique from those of the children. Parents serve as the executives of the family; their role is to provide emotional support for each other, provide nurturing and emotional support for their children, establish the rules and norms of the family, mete out the rewards for adherence to the rules and the sanctions for infractions, socialize the children, and supply the necessities of life. The role of the children, generally, is to complain about the rules; follow them anyway; absorb the rules and norms of the parents in preparation for their integration into society; develop responsibility for themselves; and, finally, grow, go, and establish their own homes. The broken line in Minuchin's scheme suggests that, despite the parents' authority in the home, children have access to their parents and can safely speak out to question rules and to request what they need. Furthermore, even in the most traditional homes where the father is the primary authority and the major

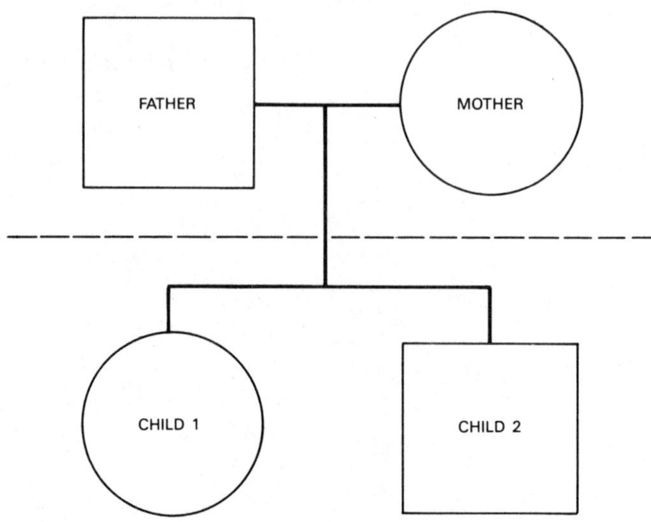

Figure 1. Structure of a Well-Functioning Family

decision maker, the mother's role with the children is highly esteemed and valued by her husband.

In the home where mother is abused, the author would alter the diagram in two ways (see Figure 2). Because the wife who is physically abused is always verbally denigrated as well, the mother in Figure 2 no longer occupies an executive position in the family. Her role is analogous to that of a child who is punished. Frequently, the father actively undermines the mother's attempts to discipline the children. For example, the mother's statement "You must stay in tonight because you haven't done your homework." may be met with the father's statement "You don't have to listen to your mother. You can go whenever you please." Hence the author has drawn an unbroken boundary in the dysfunctional home of the abused woman because her authority ceases, and she is rigidly relegated to the position of child.

The physically and/or emotionally abused wife is frequently distraught, frightened, and always very unsure of herself. The children who witness her pain, even those who are only 2 or 3 years of age, may attempt to comfort their mother. Even if they do not, she may turn to them, confide in them, and become emotionally closer to them than to her husband because he does not provide the comfort and support that she needs. The abusing husband may intensify his wife's alignment with the children by actively discouraging and even forbidding any socializing with family and friends (Star, 1980), thus denying her other social outlets. Consequently, in Figure 2, the author has also drawn a dotted line to suggest this diffusion of roles. The children take on

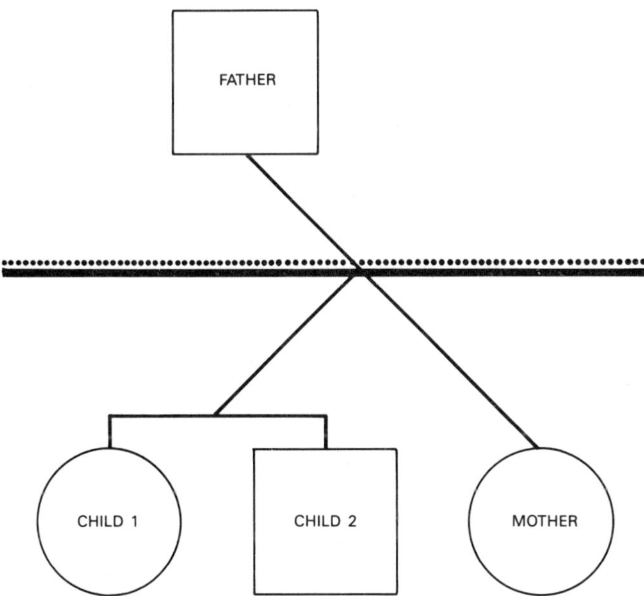

Figure 2. Structure of the Families in Which Father Abuses Mother

the roles of nurturer, care-giver, and provider of emotional support for their mother—executive roles in a well-functioning family. As the children reach their teens, their executive role may be dramatically altered from one of nurturance to one of abuse. Even adolescent daughters may verbally "push mother around" and become physically abusive (Davidson, 1978; Pressman, 1984).

In the most severe cases of abuse, the mother may handle the abuse by "psychic numbing" (Pressman, 1984). She may cope with her emotional and physical pain by involuntarily deadening her affective responses, minimizing and denying the enormity of the horror that she experiences. This emotional withdrawal and depression may render her unavailable to her children for guidance, emotional support, and even for physical needs. Consequently, in the most destructive scenarios, children from homes where the mother is abused may suffer not only emotional deprivation, but also physical neglect.

Although a wife cannot help but withdraw emotionally when she has been abused, she will still try to please her husband and will remain available as a sexual partner, a care-giver, and a homemaker. Compliance with her husband's wishes is a way of surviving and becomes a major means for avoiding abuse (Star, 1980). This approach is only partially successful, however, for no woman can end her partner's use of violence to control her. Furthermore, as compliant as she may be, he may continue to abuse her physically and will certainly continue to abuse her verbally. Whether or not he continues to abuse her physically, her compliance is a reflection of her constant fear and awareness that she must defer to him or risk physical violence or explosive verbal tirades.

EMOTIONAL CYCLE IN WIFE-ABUSED HOMES

There are several characteristic events that tend to "feed" one another when a man becomes violent toward his wife. The cycle consists of the following elements:

1. The husband becomes controlling in order to ensure that his emotional needs are met.
2. The wife is demoted in the hierarchy and, because of feelings of fear, hurt, or confusion, is less available emotionally to her husband.
3. The wife either turns to the children for fulfillment of her emotional needs or becomes emotionally deadened.
4. The children may no longer experience nurturance and protection. They are parentified, indulged, given status equal to that of mother, or neglected.
5. The father feels more isolated in the family because of the tie between the mother and the children, and he may feel more lonely. His emotional needs are not satisfactorily met. Therefore, the father controls more.

Although this cycle feeds itself, it is abundantly clear that the wife's behavior in no way keeps the husband's violence alive. Those who try to explain the violence in terms of feedback loops totally ignore the social forces, encompassing and pervasive, that endorse and foster violent behavior against women. Social institutions conspire to maintain men in positions of economic independence and power while maintaining women in economically inferior and subordinate positions (Pressman, 1984). This imbalance is especially significant in homes where wives are abused.

Goldner (1985) was particularly critical of family therapy that ignores these social realities and resists attending to facts that "threaten the reigning paradigm" (p.22). She graphically pointed out that psychological interdependence (e.g., master and slave) does not inevitably lead to a relationship in which the participants hold equal power. Goldner stated

> that when we make the wife responsible for her husband's drinking, or for her broken nose, we are not so much reframing a complex reality as we are protecting the man and blaming his wife because that way, . . ., we keep the case. . . . [This case is the] clinging to a

theoretical perspective in which power and inequality are discredited as clinical concepts because they are deemed products of "linear thinking." (p.22)

Restricting the definitions of interpersonal problems to dysfunctional sequences rather than examining the real power differentials between the sexes keeps the reality of power differentials out of the theory of family therapy.

Men who abuse women come into relationships ready to abuse as a result of powerful social forces. However compliant the wife of an abusing man becomes (e.g., satisfying her husband's every need) or however defiant (e.g., standing up for herself, but remaining in the relationship), she will be abused. Before the abuse, most of these women are emotionally responsive to their partners. Despite the warmth that their wives can offer them, battering men abuse their partners because their need is so enormous and their expectations that their partners should meet their need to feel good about themselves is so unrealistic that no partner could possibly fulfill their needs (Star, 1980).

DIAGNOSIS

Women who are abused often seek help from physicians, clergymen, social workers, and friends; however, they do not always reveal that they are being abused (Pressman, 1984). They talk of depression, anxiety, inability to sleep, and vague concerns about their marriages, particularly poor communication and lack of openness. With physicians, they may talk of genuine somatic complaints, such as gastrointestinal ailments, back pain, headaches, heart palpitations, and depression—all symptoms that may, in fact, reflect physiological responses to the trauma of abuse. It is imperative, therefore, that helping agents ask specific questions of all couples who seek their help; of all women who have psychosomatic complaints, depression, and marital concerns; and of all husbands whose wives have left or are threatening to leave. These questions, which can be very explicit and direct, should follow a natural progression, beginning with the somewhat innocuous and moving to the emotionally charged. For example, after a series of questions regarding the marriage (e.g., areas of satisfaction, areas of dissatisfaction, involvement with friends both as a couple and as individuals, involvement with parents-in-law, conflict in these areas), the helping agent can ask, "How are decisions made in the family?" "How are decisions regarding finances made?" "How is anger expressed between you and your partner?" "Does anyone express anger physically, such as by throwing objects, hitting walls, pushing a partner, pulling hair, hitting, kicking, or punching?"

A therapist's awareness of violence in a client's family of origin, either against the client's mother or against the client as a child, generates likely hypotheses about the client's functioning and beliefs. A woman with such a history, for example, probably feels helpless, believes that she has no control over her life, and is more disposed to caring for and nurturing others than to holding any expectations for herself. Such attitudes are consistent with the ways in which women are traditionally socialized, and a woman who has known violence in her family of origin is much less likely to be influenced by changing mores and much more likely to believe that violence is a norm.

A man with a history of abuse in his family of origin is likely to abuse his partner either verbally or physically, as 80% of men who witnessed abuse or were abused themselves as children abuse their partners (Rosenbaum & O'Leary, 1981; Roy, 1977). Furthermore, these men generally are distrustful of others, do not allow themselves to become close to other people, are secretive, and strongly believe that their lives and problems are no one else's business.

Once it has been established that a wife is being abused, it is essential to determine the frequency and severity of the violence, as well as to acquire other information. The husband and wife must be interviewed separately, because the wife's discussion of her concerns in her husband's presence may render her extremely vulnerable when she returns home with him. Also, she may be very fearful in her husband's presence and feel much more comfortable discussing the abuse apart from him.

In the course of the separate assessment interviews, the therapist should explore information regarding the husband's family of origin to help both the husband and the wife make sense of behavior that is extremely distressing to both of them. The therapist should ask both partners specific questions about the methods of control used by the husband's parents and about a history of violence in the husband's family of origin. For the husband, a declaration that he was reared in a violent environment helps him recognize that he is not a monster, but has learned such behavior. Similarly, his father is not a monster, but probably learned his style in his original family. Making the link between childhood learning and current behavior also helps the husband realize that he is responsible for his violent behavior, not his wife.

For the wife, the realization that her husband's violent behavior has grown out of his childhood experiences helps her curtail the tendency to blame herself for his behavior (Star, 1980). Because women are generally socialized to believe that they are responsible for the emotional well-being of all family members, abused women often believe that if they loved better, "got it right," their husbands would not hurt them. Even when they recognize that their husbands' violence arises from childhood experiences or stress and frustrations apart from themselves, they feel responsible for helping their husbands "get better." Therapists must make it clear that abused wives cannot change their partners, only the ways in which they cope with their partners' violence and the ways in which they attend to their own safety.

Just as it is typical for abused wives to internalize blame, it is typical for abusing men to externalize blame (Ganley, 1981). Men may hold their partner responsible for their abusive behavior because "she pushes me too far," "she nags," or "she provokes me." Violent men must recognize that wives may behave in ways that make their husbands angry, but that husbands can respond to such behavior in a consciously planned way rather than in an impulsive, emotionally charged way. In Bowen's terms (1978), abusing men are described as highly "undifferentiated" and, consequently, tend to respond emotionally rather than thoughtfully. They must learn to recognize their feelings, to assess the situations that give rise to those feelings, and to think rationally of ways to express those feelings—ways that are nonviolent, nonaggressive, and nonhurtful to others.

Although the therapist should not necessarily ask the husband about the wife's family of origin, it is critical to explore with the wife her family of origin and the possible presence of violence there. If her father occupied the dominant role in the family and maintained a position of power by keeping his wife and children financially dependent on him and socially isolated from extrafamilial relationships (Sgroi, 1982), the therapist should investigate the possibility of incest. The wife who is an incest survivor, but has not received counseling for the sexual abuse, is likely to see herself as powerless and unable to control her own life. Furthermore, she commonly views others as unlikely to provide her protection or assistance against abuse (Gelinas, 1983). Such a woman needs a great deal of help (e.g., individual therapy, a support group) to make sense of the sexual abuse that she experienced as a child and its effects on her current ways of viewing herself and the world about her.

Because the family dynamics in the wife-abused home are comparable to those in an incest family, it is vital for a therapist who treats wife abuse to be on the alert for sexual abuse of the children. When either the wife or the husband has become engaged in counseling, the therapist must explore the effects of the wife abuse on the children and inquire about signs of such sexual abuse (Sgroi, 1982):

- a sudden drop in school performance
- lack of trust, particularly with significant others
- hints about sexual activity
- persistent and inappropriate sexual play with peers, with toys, or with themselves
- sexually aggressive behavior with others

- detailed and age-inappropriate understanding of sexual behavior, especially by young children
- running away from home
- sleep disturbances

When children from violent homes attend meetings for support groups or conjoint sessions with their mother, they can be asked directly about all forms of abuse.

TREATMENT OF ABUSING MEN

Several essential issues for violent men can be addressed by family-of-origin therapy:

- developing empathic responses
- identifying child-rearing beliefs learned in childhood
- identifying attitudes regarding male-female roles and expectations learned in childhood
- learning to express feelings other than anger
- developing trust in others
- becoming open about themselves
- accepting responsibility for abusing behavior

Men who abuse their partners lack empathy. Despite their own typical history of abuse, they have no sense of the pain that they inflict either on those who directly experience their abuse or on those who witness it. Because abusing men have generally lacked fathers who are nurturing and responsive to their partners, they seal off in themselves a well of feelings that they consider feminine or vulnerable (e.g., fear, hurt, sadness, uncertainty) and are, therefore, unable to identify with such feelings in others. The experience of reliving their own childhoods allows them access to those early feelings of victimization and, thereby, to a capacity for appreciating the feelings in their wives who have been abused by them. These men do love their partners and do not feel good about their violence. They are not a sociopathic population (Straus, Gelles, & Steinmetz, 1980).

Like so many men in our society, battering men are comfortable expressing only "manly" feelings, and the prime "manly" feelings are anger and aggression. It is imperative, therefore, that battering men learn not only to identify feelings other than anger, but also to express them. Journeys into the past can elicit a range of such feelings that must be thoroughly explored. The act of "opening up" through the therapist's probing question is also the beginning of trust. Ideally, therapy for abusers should occur in a group format, as openness before the group further encourages such trust.

Although battering husbands do not necessarily abuse their children, they may be particularly harsh and punitive fathers. This tendency reflects their own fathers' highly punitive attitudes. Questions about the nurturing and disciplining style of adults, as parents and/or as partners; the use of violence; and their understanding of their parents' methods help abusers develop new beliefs and attitudes regarding the role of discipline, appropriate forms of discipline, and the need for fathers/husbands to be nurturing.

In general, the therapist asks abusing men to return to their childhoods and to recall relationships among family members, such as to whom did family members turn for support, who comforted abusers as children, who disciplined abusers as children, and how. The therapist must also ask whether the men were physically or sexually abused, whether they sexually abused other family members, and whether anyone else abused other family members. Invariably, a litany of very painful memories emerges. In response, the men first defend their parents behavior, saying that they deserved to be beaten, strapped, or soundly punched. As the therapist has challenged their use of violence against their wives and their justification of it, however, the therapist challenges the violence of their fathers.

In making this challenge, the therapist should be very careful never to denigrate the parent or in any way to take the valued image of this parent from the client. Instead, the therapist may suggest that, just as the client has learned from his father, his father learned from his parents. The therapist may point out that the client's parents were acting in what they believed to be the best interest of their children and intended no harm. At this point, the men become aware of the loss of nurturing childhood experiences that would have made them feel safe and protected, nourished and valued.

With the therapist, the men consider then what they wish had happened in their childhoods and examine these wishes in the light of their own children's needs. The therapist also asks them to explore what they remember of their mothers' responses to their fathers' abusive behavior and what they felt for their mothers when they witnessed the abuse. Finally, the therapist asks them to review when they left home and the circumstances under which they left.

TREATMENT OF ABUSED WOMEN

In the treatment of women who have been abused, there are other issues that family-of-origin therapy can address:

- exploring possible signs of incest
- reviewing societal values conveyed in the home that keep a wife feeling helpless and obliged to aid a partner who is needy
- identifying learned functions and rules for a wife and mother, particularly those that women must give and give in order to receive love (family rules)
- becoming comfortable in expressing feelings and developing characteristics regarded as unfeminine (e.g., anger, neediness, assertiveness)
- identifying child-rearing concepts learned in childhood
- recognizing a woman's right to expectations for herself
- examining the nature of family responses when a woman confides in family members as an adult

Unlike abusing men, abused women may have no history of abuse in their families of origin. In fact, the battered women whom Walker (1977-1978) studied tended to describe a benign, paternalistic "Dresden doll" type of upbringing in which they learned very early that only their competence in the social area would be useful to them in life. An exploration of the values and rules that they acquired in their early lives is extremely useful in helping these women recognize the influence of these values and rules on the decisions that they are making about their abusive relationships.

A great part of therapy with battered women involves challenging the rules and societal myths that predispose battered women to remain in relationships that are not only physically unsafe, but also extremely destructive to their children (Elbow, 1982; Jaffe, Wolfe, Wilson, & Zak, 1986; Sopp-Gibson, 1980). These myths, which are global in nature, have been expressed by non-abused women as follows:

- "My needs come after family needs are met."
- "Mother makes or breaks the home. She is the center of the home."
- "Good mothers never say, No!"
- "If things go wrong, you are at fault. Mothers are a good place to take garbage."
- "Mothers have all the answers or should know all the answers."

Many women believe that they will be loved only if they give love. Consequently, they transmit signals that fairly shout, "I am here to give to you and love you; come and take from me!" Because battering men are among the neediest of people, they are drawn to these nurturing women. It is not uncommon for battered women who leave one battering relationship to enter another one. These women usually indicate that they did not experience the abuse before making a commitment to the relationship or, if they did, the men were so remorseful and contrite that the women responded to their pain. These women in no way are seeking battering relationships, it is their willingness to give that attracts needy men, and this neediness attracts nurturing women.

In general, it is very difficult for women to ask for what they themselves need. Exploring their families of origin in therapy, abused women "discover" the roles that their mothers have served: namely, they have put others' needs before their own and have considered it selfish to ask that their own needs be met. Women must learn that they need to replenish themselves and that being nurtured is as great a human need as nurturing others.

When women turn to their families for support after deciding either to remain in an abusive relationship or to leave, the therapist should explore the nature of that support and the kind of messages that family members, especially parents, are conveying. Some parents have failed to support a daughter who decided to leave a partner unwilling to seek help because the husband was so despondent, so tearfully pained at the loss, and so repentent. These parents have no concept of the pain that a battered woman suffers nor of the abusing husband's tendency to break promises. Friends and family sometimes encourage abused women to leave the "cursed dogs," but they have no concept of the ambivalence that battered women feel.

The family-of-origin questions for women delve into what the family rules regarding male-female expectations and codes of behavior were; to whom the children in the family turned for support; to whom the adults turned for support and comfort; what the family believed about separation and commitment; whether the battered women have been parentified and, therefore, expect to continue to nurture and serve almost exclusively as adults; when they left home; and under what circumstances did they leave.

CONCLUSION

Reviewing family-of-origin histories and family-of-origin patterns helps both abusing men and abused women reassess the benefits and shortcomings of their childhood learning, helps them reexperience and resolve the hurt and anger generated by early experiences, increases their understanding of the needs and expectations ascribed to men and women, and affords them the opportunity to form new beliefs and new family patterns.

REFERENCES

Bowen, M. (1978). *Family therapy in clinical practice*. New York. Jason Aronson.

Davidson, T. (1978). *Conjugal crime: Understanding and changing the wifebeating pattern*. New York: Ballantine Books.

Elbow, M. (1982). Children of violent marriages: The forgotten victims. *Social Casework, 63,* 465–471.

Ganley, A.L. (1981). *Court-mandated counseling for men who batter: A three-day workshop for mental health professionals.* Washington, DC: The Center for Women Policy Studies.

Gelinas, D.J. (1983). The persisting negative effects of incest. *Psychiatry, 46,* 312–332.

Goldner, V. (1985). Warning: Family therapy may be hazardous to your health. *Family Therapy Networker, 9,* 19–23.

Jaffe, P., Wolfe, D., Wilson, S., & Zak, L. (1986). Similarities in behavioral and social maladjustment among child victims and witnesses to family violence. *American Journal of Orthopsychiatry, 56,* 142–146.

Minuchin, S. (1974). *Families and family therapy.* Cambridge, MA: Harvard University Press.

Pressman, B.M. (1984). *Family violence: Origins and treatment.* Guelph, Ontario: Office For Educational Practice, University of Guelph.

Rosenbaum, A., & O'Leary, K.D. (1981). Children: The unintended victims of marital violence. *American Journal of Orthopsychiatry, 51,* 692–699.

Roy, M. (1977). *Battered women.* New York: Von Nostrand Reinhold.

Sgroi, S.M. (1982). *Handbook of clinical intervention in child sexual abuse.* Lexington, MA: D.C. Heath.

Sopp-Gibson, S. (1980). Children from violent homes. *Journal, Ontario Association of Children's Aid Societies, 23,* 1–5, 10.

Star, B. (1980). Patterns in family violence. *Social Casework, 61,* 339–346.

Straus, M.A., Gelles, R.J., & Steinmetz, S.K. (1980). *Behind closed doors: Violence in the American family.* Garden City, NY: Anchor Press/Doubleday.

Walker, L.E. (1977-1978). Battered women and learned helplessness. *Victimology: An International Journal, 2,* 525–534.

6. Family-of-Origin Therapy within Sex Therapy

Claude A. Guldner, ThD
Professor in Charge
Child and Family Services Research Unit
Associate Professor
Department of Family Studies
University of Guelph
Guelph, Ontario

The treatment of sexual problems and dysfunctions was generally the province of psychiatry before 1970. Following the publication of *Human Sexual Inadequacy* (Masters & Johnson, 1970), however, sex therapy took a major turn. As a result, the length of time required for sex therapy was shortened to 10 or 12 weekly sessions or within a 2-week period. Therapy consisted of a combination of in-session communication experiences and out-of-session behavioral sessions designed to alleviate anxiety and spectatoring. The sessions focused primarily on a modification of the client's attitudes about sexuality. Gradually, clinicians realized that not all cases lend themselves to this treatment format, and other theories and models emerged. The more significant of these are the approach of Kaplan (1974), who advocated treatment from a combination of systems and psychodynamic perspectives; the behavioral approaches of LoPiccolo and Lobitz (1972), as well as that of Annon (1976); the cognitive approach of Ellis (1980); and the group treatment formats of Barbach (1975, 1980) and Zilbergeld (1980).

As sex therapy moved into the 1980s, most clinicians were seeing fewer of the standard sexual dysfunctions (e.g., premature ejaculation, anorgasmy, vaginismus, dyspareunia) and more sexual problems that originated in the particular systemic dynamics of the marital dyad and of the extended family. For example, secondary erectile dysfunctions, secondary orgasmic dysfunctions, low desire and low arousal, and, in many instances, ejaculatory incompetence are reflections of complex systemic stress in the couple; the couple is stalled in the developmental life cycle, and/or recursive systemic patterns from the family of origin are being replayed in the current nuclear family. These clients may present a sexual problem to a therapist, or the sexual difficulties may emerge from the clients' description of marital and/or family complaints. Such sexual problems require treatment procedures that are longer and more complex than are those available in the brief format of earlier approaches to sex therapy.

Increasingly, the literature is suggesting that the distinction between marital therapy and sex therapy is artificial and does not reflect what clinicians observe in their practice. Sager (1976) found a mixture of marital and sexual problems in almost 75% of the couples whom he treated. Watters, Askwith, Cohen, and Lamont (1985) said that the split between "marital" and "sexual" therapies is anachronistic because it symbolizes the alienation that was once believed to exist between an individual's sexuality and his or her personality as a whole.

Family-of-origin therapy has generally been seen as the antithesis of brief therapy. Family-of-origin therapy takes place over a longer time span. The frequent sessions of the early stages give way to sessions that have longer time periods between them to allow for the performance of out-of-session tasks. In a sense, the therapist attempts to help the client change a lifelong emotional pattern. This cannot be done by following a few behavioral modification homework tasks.

At first glance, it may seem impossible to combine sex therapy with family-of-origin therapy, as they come from such diverse backgrounds. Often, however, it is necessary to combine the two models in order to obtain the most lasting resolution of the problem. The area of human sexuality is highly charged with emotion. Few families have been comfortable dealing with developmental issues that involve sexuality. In most families, one's sexuality is a private or even taboo topic. Most family members know virtually nothing about the sexual behaviors of other family members. Family attitudes about sexuality are often assumed on the basis of major or minor incidents, or generalized (usually as negative). Many clients who have sexual problems find it helpful just to talk as an *adult* with members of their family of origin regarding sexuality. This change in the communication pattern of the family of origin often has significant effects on the communication pattern of the current family.

CRITERIA FOR APPROPRIATENESS OF FAMILY-OF-ORIGIN THERAPY

Five criteria may be used to assess the appropriateness of family-of-origin therapy for a client with a sexual problem:

1. The marriage and/or sexual relationship has enough conflict or pain to sustain motivation, but is not so intense that family-of-origin treatment will exacerbate problems in either partner.
2. The client recognizes and understands the systemic basis of current conflicts and does not take an individual or linear view of causality.
3. The client and the therapist have identified issues that make it difficult for the client to attain a position of differentiation in the current system as well as in past systems, such as fusion or emotional cut-offs.
4. The client has a relationship with the extended family system, time, energy, and a life style that permit the client to perform out-of-session tasks and to give priority to family-of-origin work.
5. Both spouses are committed at a relatively equal level to working on family-of-origin issues along with their sexual complaints. Without this consistency, family-of-origin therapy may create an imbalance in the couple's goals. The partner not involved in the family-of-origin work becomes impatient and resistive when sex therapy is delayed. Furthermore, because spouses function at approximately the same level of differentiation, both spouses have issues that can be addressed in family-of-origin work.

TREATMENT STEPS

The first step in the family-of-origin process is to construct a thorough genogram. It takes at least one full session for each partner to present his or her genogram and for the therapist to identify the significant information in it. The genograms enable the therapist to assist each client in connecting the past to the present and to the future. This process generally produces the goals for the early family-of-origin sessions. In addition, it often reveals what must take place before the client can gain the differentiation necessary to resolve the sexual problem.

The genogram-focused sessions are conducted with both partners present. As one partner unfolds his or her genogram, the other takes the role of participant-observer, commenting or adding information from time to time, but essentially remaining in the background while the partner shares information with the therapist. This process establishes a structure for the family-of-origin sessions with marital partners. Most of the sessions are divided, with half the time spent on each partner. At the end of each segment, the other partner has an opportunity to make a brief commentary. The therapist permits only additional observations in these commentaries, not interpretations or processing of material.

The therapist should spend the early sessions preparing the clients attitudinally for family-of-origin intervention. It is important for clients to realize that they are not entering past systems to change others, but rather to understand the system, especially its patterns of triangles and the projection process, and to learn to take a different position—that is, a more differentiated position—within that system.

As the next step in treatment, the therapist may ask couples who are comfortable working with a more cognitive framework to do a writing task as described below. This technique was originally developed as a training tool for sex therapists, but its increasing use with clients has revealed that it has important benefits in treatment. It serves as an extension of the genogram in that it identifies and highlights family patternings around the theme of sexuality.

One instrument that may be used in this writing task is called *Exploration of My Personal Sexual Script* (Guldner, 1980). It is divided into two sections of 15 questions each. The first section focuses on family system influences and provides a fairly adequate picture of relationship patterns, sex differences and expectations, projections, emotional cut-offs, and triangles. The second section, called a personal analysis, focuses more on current patterns, specifically those that are related to sexuality and sexual functioning. Clients may spend as much or as little time as they wish with the instrument. Most put a great deal of effort into it; the average length of these written documents is 20 to 25 pages.

In the therapy sessions, clients select four or five key relationship issues from the script analysis; these become the basis for out-of-session task assignments. Once this is done, the therapist asks them to decide if they would benefit from sharing the material with their partner. If they agree, the therapist instructs the partner to read the material essentially from an objective position. Most clients indicate that reading their partner's written descriptions gives them a clearer picture of the past's connection to the present behavior and attitudes of their partner. This further enhances the differentiation of the present system.

Family-of-origin therapy involves clients in a gradual learning process that enables them to understand their family as a system and the unique part that they play in that system. Therefore, interventions are designed to enhance this process. The early work consists of gaining the cooperation of the clients as researchers into their own family backgrounds. They may extend their genogram data by obtaining information from important others in the family. By means of this procedure, clients begin to get a picture of the seven *R*s of the family:

1. the family's *roots,* that is, multigenerational history
2. the different *roles* that members took within the family
3. the family's *rhythms,* for example, space, time, and context events that influenced roles
4. the *rules* that developed in the family and the extent to which they originated in previous generations or evolved in the current family patterning

5. the family *routines,* the particular patterning that family members developed
6. the family *rituals,* that is, the more formalized events in the ongoing life of the family
7. the *relationship* patterns of dyads, triangles, and interlocking triangles

When clients have a fairly good understanding of these data, the therapist intervenes in an effort to make new patterns of contact with family members. Generally, such interventions initially involve those family members who evoke less anxiety in the clients. At first, the client discusses individual family members independently of one another. This later gives way to dyads in which the clients come to understand the triangulating process and their part in it.

The treatment session focuses on making sense of these data and learning to take a more objective position in regard to both the data and the relationships from which the data emerge. The clients are coached to think from an "I" position rather than a "you" or "we" position.

CASE EXAMPLE

The sexual dysfunctions of low desire and low arousal are frequently associated with unfinished business from the family of origin. Low desire dysfunctions are generally described in terms of differences between the frequency with which individuals in a relationship desire sexual activity. Low arousal concerns the level of subjective excitement that individuals experience while participating in sexual activity. Often, it is not enough simply to identify the past influences that have contributed to a problem; it is necessary to take therapeutic action to help clients gain emotional liberation from past family injunctions.

> Jay and Karen were referred from the outpatient department of a psychiatric facility for marital and sexual therapy. Both had been hospitalized for a brief period about 6 months earlier, and they had been seen individually as outpatients since that time. During the first session, the couple described the deterioration of their marriage over the past 3 years. Companionship was minimal, there was very little sharing, and the relationship had no affectional and sexual elements. At the same time, both were committed to maintaining the marriage.
>
> Jay and Karen had been married for 9 years; however, they had known each other for 13 years and had lived together for 2 years before marriage. During those 2 years, Karen experienced vag-

inismus, and the couple did not have intercourse. Jay indicated that he had been somewhat disappointed, but that he valued companionship more than he needed sex. Following their marriage, Jay and Karen undertook more sexual exploration, as they both wanted to have a child. Gradually, Karen relaxed sufficiently to make intercourse possible. Jay stated, however, that she was always passive and that sex was never as enjoyable to him as he had fantasized it should be. They had a child 2 years after their marriage and did not engage in sexual activity more than once a month or, at times, once every 2 or 3 months from that time onward. They had a second child 2 years before they entered therapy and did not resume sexual intercourse or show any physical affection following the birth of the second child.

Approximately a year before treatment, Jay had become depressed. Two weeks before he was hospitalized for depression, he left Karen a note that he needed space and time by himself, and moved out of the home. Karen was devastated by this step. Finding that she could not keep food down, she was hospitalized in a general hospital and then transferred to the same psychiatric hospital that Jay had entered. Both were placed on medication and supportive outpatient therapy, then referred for marital treatment with an underlying sexual problem.

In the early assessment sessions with the couple, it became clear that Karen was strongly fused with Jay and that this pattern reflected her enmeshed family of origin. On the other hand, Jay had made an emotional cut-off from his family at the age of 16, when he moved out of the family home and got a job. He had maintained this pattern in subsequent systems. Even after he became the owner of a very successful business and hired his two brothers to work in the business, he did not interact socially with his family of origin. Only after the birth of his children did he begin to have social contact with his parents. Even then, he tended to be reserved, allowing Karen to be the go-between for himself and his family.

It was obvious that standard sexual therapy was not appropriate for this couple. The problems in the relationship originated in unfinished business in the couple's families of origin. When the therapist suggested that they enter family-of-origin therapy, Jay liked the idea, but Karen was not so willing. After observing a demonstration of family-of-origin work in which family sculpting techniques were used, however, both Jay and Karen felt that the therapist had precisely identified their family pattern. They made a commitment to working within a family-of-origin framework.

The genogram revealed that Karen saw her family as a highly enmeshed group with a great many overlapping triangles. She felt that she was her parents' favorite child and her brothers' favorite sister. She was close to her sister, yet she and her sister formed competitive triangles whenever they were with anyone else in the family. Everyone in the family was very verbal, and there was little internal privacy. Dyadic interaction in the family was minimal, and Karen sensed a general attitude that the privilege of others in the family had been violated whenever two people were alone together. Karen moved out of her family home only after she had made a firm connection with Jay, who was the only man she had seriously dated.

As the youngest in his family of origin, Jay saw himself as "mother's baby," and he believed her smothering drove him to his emotional cut-off from the family at 16. "It was a survival tactic," he said. He saw his father as distant and uninvolved in the family, as were his older brothers. Because his sister played the role of pseudo-mother with him, he felt that he had "two women leading my life." Jay had been attracted to Karen initially not only because she was attractive, but also because she was outgoing and verbal. He complained, however, that she smothered him.

Karen and Jay performed several tasks during the year of family-of-origin therapy. For example, the therapist instructed Karen to stop being the go-between for Jay and his family. Jay's mother called Karen and Jay nearly every day to see how they were, especially Jay. Karen usually handled these calls, providing information about the family and Jay's work. Although Karen found it difficult to talk with her mother-in-law only about herself and to explain that information about Jay would have to come from him, she was relieved to be rid of this triangulated position in the intergenerational system. Karen's action caused Jay to become quite anxious, but his anxiety maintained his motivation to work with his family-of-origin issues.

For the most part, Karen worked at differentiation by creating a new position for herself within her family of origin. She took time to get to know each family member as a unique individual. When she was with her family, she learned to observe the triangulation process and to recognize her own participation in it. The therapist helped her to realize that she would fall into old patterns of relating when she became anxious. Identifying this process enabled Karen to gain more objectivity and remain more emotionally free of the triangulation process. When her brother developed cancer, Karen was able to take a supportive and yet more removed position within the family context. She felt this was a major transition point for her in her family differentiation process. She returned to her previous job as a special education teacher on a part-time basis, feeling that it gave her a personal fulfillment quite apart from Jay.

Jay began his family-of-origin work with his father. He felt most distant from his father, yet safe with him. They had no specific task except to get to know one another. Thus, he invited his father to take business trips with him so that they would have time to talk. Jay, his father, and his two brothers went on a fishing trip together. The reminiscence of childhood made Jay interested in learning more about his brothers' perceptions of life. He began to interact with each of them at a more personal and feeling level. Approximately 5 months into treatment, he began to take the telephone calls from his mother. Sometimes, he would tell her that he did not have time to talk, however. At first, he was guilty and depressed over this, but he gradually learned to handle the calls in a more objective manner.

Jay's major work came in extricating himself from the triangle of his mother, his father, and himself. He had always resented his father for not protecting him from the demands of his mother. In the early stages of therapy, he would sometimes become preoccupied with this and would react by distancing himself from Karen and complaining that she was too demanding. He gradually learned to identify this pattern and began to take a more objective stance, seeing the parental pattern and accepting it without anger. His ability to allow his parents their own relationship was especially facilitated when he took time to talk with them individually about their past families. He came to understand his mother's position better when he realized that, as the oldest daughter in an Italian family of nine children, she was given responsibility early and expected to help rear her siblings. "She has been in charge since she was 8 years old," he reported.

The impact of this family-of-origin work on the marriage was significant. In the early stages, Jay did not believe that Karen could change; whenever she appeared less needy of his connection, he would express his doubt that the change was real. Perceiving no change in his mother's controlling behavior through the years, he concluded that his wife—who demonstrated much the same behavior—also could not change. One pattern that Jay and Karen had followed during most of their marriage was that of the pursuer and the distancer (Fogarty, 1979). Karen's need for closeness to gain emotional fulfillment of herself led her to want so much of Jay that it was akin to fusion. As she moved closer, Jay would take the position of the distancer, closing down both emotionally and physically to protect his own space. This pattern changed dramatically during therapy. Karen could express her need to Jay, but Jay was not her only source of support. As she needed less of him, he was willing to stay in closer contact with her.

Before the couple's family-of-origin work, Jay underfunctioned in terms of identifying and expressing feelings. Karen, however, overfunctioned in that she interpreted not only her own feelings, but also Jay's feelings. Thus, Karen gained a sense of worth by taking care of Jay at the personal feeling level. Jay cooperated in this process by letting Karen "tell him" what he was experiencing and what he needed to do. He then became angry at her overinvolvement and accused her of control, further distancing himself. The more Jay worked with his family-of-origin material, the more he was able to identify his own feelings and to communicate those feelings. Recognizing that all the members of her family of origin believed that they understood each other intuitively, Karen decided to stop this mind reading process with Jay. She asked him to share and felt it deepened their communication when he did. When he did not, she learned to accept it without reacting "at the emotional level of a denied child," as she put it.

As the marriage improved, so did the sexual relationship. Karen realized that her early vaginismus was symbolic of her inability to allow Jay into her space. Although she loved him, he was still an outsider. Jay had tolerated her inability to have intercourse, because it allowed him to keep his distance. "Distance was more important than sex," he said. After marriage, Karen felt more trusting of Jay as an outsider; she relaxed, and intercourse was possible. Jay noted that, before the second pregnancy, he had been detaching himself from their sexual experiences. Following the birth, when the frequency of their sexual experiences diminished, he protected his masculine image by believing that sex was another means that Karen used to control him. Also, he accused her of being a passive and uninteresting sex partner. Although she was enjoying sex more, she did not want to threaten the relationship by seeking more. She needed Jay's presence more than she needed a satisfying sexual relationship.

Approximately 8 months into treatment, Jay and Karen began to show more affection toward one another. This was followed by a report that they were involved in more frequent intercourse. In the 10th month, Karen reexamined the sexual scripts that they had written and noted that neither of them had known how to develop a positive sexual relationship. They both indicated a need for information and guidance in improving their sexual contacts. The therapist asked them to read a book about sexual expression in marriage, showed them a set of slides about the sexual response cycle, and gave them permission to be experimental and creative in sexual contact.

At that time, the therapist discussed with them the impact of their past attitudes on their current behavior and instructed them to meta-communicate about their sexual feelings and needs. This process enabled them to clarify what they each wanted from sexual contact. They learned to be clear in their initiation of sexual contact and to refuse when uninterested.

When treatment was terminated, both Jay and Karen had developed more satisfying positions within their families of origin. They perceived their individual and shared visits with both families as generally positive. In their own marriage, there was an increase in conflict, but they saw this as positive. Their ability to maintain a more differentiated position enabled them to resolve issues. Both companionship and sharing had increased. The frequency of sexual relations was now at least once a week and sometimes more, with either initiating it. Jay was accepting of Karen's more active role in the relationship, and they were both open to experimentation. Although much more might have been done with this couple to enhance differentiation, it was outside the initial treatment goal of creating a more satisfying marital and sexual relationship.

CONCLUSION

Family-of-origin work is *not* an exploration or interpretation of the past. Rather, it is a means of freeing the client from entanglements that may have sources in the past, but are active and alive in both the nuclear and extended family systems in the present. Perhaps more than any other interpersonal issue, sexuality confronts the individual with what Bowen (1978) considered the forces that strive for togetherness within the family and the forces that lead to separateness and autonomy. Individuals must come to terms with themselves as autonomous sexual beings. Individuals who have not achieved adequate self differentiation within their family of origin are potential candidates for sexual conflicts and/or dysfunctions.

Our society has imbued human sexuality with so much emotionality that virtually no individual growing up in this century can discriminate intellectual from emotional functioning in the sexual area. Most people lack adequate information regarding human sexual functioning to use cognitive processes and, thus, easily fall back on emotionally laden messages. Furthermore, the family reinforcement of the cultural messages regarding sexuality, interwoven with other elements of the family emotional system, increases the likelihood of fusion between the intellectual and emotional functions where sexual issues are concerned. The client who does family-of-origin work as part of sex therapy not only must reestablish contact with the family of origin as a means of reducing residual anxiety, but also must expand this to other systems of society that have been purveyors of sexual messages, overtly or covertly.

REFERENCES

Annon, J.S. (1976). *The behavioral treatment of sexual problems: Brief therapy*. New York: Harper & Row.

Barbach, L.G. (1975). *For yourself: The fulfillment of female sexuality*. New York: Doubleday.

Barbach, L.G. (1980). *Women discover orgasm*. New York: Free Press.

Bowen, M. (1978). *Family therapy in clinical practice*. New York: Jason Aronson.

Ellis, A. (1980). Treatment of erectile dysfunction. In S.R. Leiblum & L.A. Pervin (Eds.), *Principles and practice of sex therapy* (pp. 234–262). New York: Guilford Press.

Fogarty, T. (1979). The distancer and the pursuer. *The Family, 1*, 11–16.

Guldner, C.A. (1980). Exploration of my personal sexual script. Available from the author, Department of Family Studies, University of Guelph, Guelph, Ontario N1G 2W1.

Kaplan, H.S. (1974). *The new sex therapy*. New York: Brunner/Mazel.

LoPiccolo, J., & Lobitz, W.C. (1972). The role of masturbation in the treatment of orgasmic dysfunction. *Archives of Sexual Behavior, 2*, 163–171.

Masters, W.H., & Johnson, V.E. (1970). *Human sexual inadequacy*. Boston: Little, Brown.

Sager, C.J. (1976). The role of sex therapy in marital therapy. *American Journal of Psychiatry, 1335*, 555–558.

Watters, W.W., Askwith, J., Cohen, M., & Lamont, J.A. (1985). An assessment approach to couples with sexual problems. *Canadian Journal of Psychiatry, 30*, 2–11.

Zilbergeld, B. (1980). Alternatives to couples counselling for sex problems: Group and individual therapy. *Journal of Sex and Marital Therapy, 6*, 3–18.

7. Family-of-Origin and Family Therapy Considerations with Black Families

Joseph R. Morris, PhD
Assistant Professor and Director
Counseling Psychology Program
Department of Counselor Education and Counseling Psychology
Western Michigan University
Kalamazoo, Michigan

Many of the recent advances in family and family-of-origin therapy have not been of particular value to large numbers of Black Americans, even though these individuals, couples, and families are frequently most in need of such therapy. Because family therapists are likely to be middle-class white individuals or aspire to higher socioeconomic status, many of the training programs for family therapists, case studies published in the academic literature, and workshops are aimed toward the concerns of clients with similar backgrounds and/or aspirations (Framo, 1981). Clearly, there is a general paucity of information that addresses family therapy intervention with Black families. More specifically, however, there is a theoretical and therapeutic void regarding family-of-origin issues with Black families. This void is unfortunate, because the family of origin has a somewhat different connotation or effect for Black families than it has for White families.

BLACK FAMILIES

Much attention has been focused on the problems of contemporary Black families. To be sure, divorce and abortion rates, female-headed households, limited employment opportunities, and geographical shifts in the job market have affected all American families; there is an urgent need to address the way in which these problems relate to Black families, however, because they may deal a fatal blow to families already troubled by financial difficulties and basic survival issues.

However well-intentioned, much of the scholarly literature and popular attention directed toward the Black family has been simply descriptive of the symptoms that arise from a deeply rooted sense of hopelessness and despair born of the everyday realities of Black life in America. It is necessary not only to explore all facets of the problem, but also to devote an equal amount of time to strategies that will ensure a more viable and self-sustaining Black family unit. Perhaps part of the problem emanates from a lack of accurate information about the more salient aspects of Black family life.

Unique Aspects of Black Family Life

Black families are best seen within the context of African family systems that emphasize "continual flexibility in circularity" (Nobles, 1974). African family interactional patterns include mutual support and kinshiplike relatedness to many members of a community, as well as egalitarian and flexible sex roles. For example, the most dependable and consistent source of financial support in Black homes may be the woman. In contrast, White families tend to have more rigid and restrictive rules in regard to the roles, functions, and behaviors of individuals within the family unit.

Many Black families have an extensive network of blood and nonblood relatives who provide the resources that allow them to overcome many obstacles and survive (Hare & Hare, 1984). Frequently, these families seek and receive assistance from members of the parents' families of origin. Unlike White families, Black families are much more likely to depend on such intergenerational ties for economic and psychological support on a wide range of important family matters.

> A young, recently married Black man refused to accept an important promotion and geographical transfer without the advice and approval of his grandfather. The wife complained that "the old man" should not be put in a position to hinder their socioeconomic advancement, especially since the grandfather had not completed elementary school. Obviously concerned about the potential employer's long, unwritten list of promises, the husband quietly insisted that his grandfather knew people better than either one of them!

The statistics with a direct bearing on the vitality of Black families are frightening and so overwhelming that many have given up any hope of the Black family's survival. In 1980, approximately 40% of all Black American households were headed by single women, 86% of Black youth lived in poverty, and 46% to 52% of Black teen-agers (i.e., aged 16–19), were unemployed (U.S. Bureau of Census, 1986). While there are indeed many complex issues facing a significant number of Black families today, the therapist can seriously err by stereotyping all Black families as disintegrating, unstable, and pathological (McAdoo, 1977). There are successful single- and two-parent families in the Black community that have developed the wherewithal to maintain a positive view of themselves while simultaneously enjoying economic, social, and, often, professional mobility. Their values and attitudes resemble those held by middle-class White clients.

Low-income Black clients may hold values that differ from those of both middle-class Whites and middle-class Blacks. Therapists may perceive the tardiness of low-income Black clients as resistance, for example, while it may only reflect a difference in time orientation between the therapist and the client (Brannon, 1983). Many White therapists claim that Black clients frequently behave in a "paranoid fashion." In reality, this "healthy skepticism" may only be a sign of good mental health in a majority culture that erects so many obstacles to psychological certainty.

• In order to become educated and upwardly mobile, many Blacks must separate physically and emotionally from members of their family of origin and extended family (McAdoo, 1977). Although this kind of isolation from the family of origin and other community support systems, coupled with a need to continue achieving, can create enormous pressure for Blacks (McAdoo, 1977), such stress may be required to sustain hard-earned economic independence and social status.

It is important for a family therapist who works with Black families to have a clear understanding of Bowen's (1978) concepts of the "differentiation of self" (i.e., the establishment of the individual's separate identity and goals that are minimally influenced by others) and the extended family "emotional system." While some "fusion" with others is reasonable and expected, particularly in marriages, difficulties in the marital relationship may result from intense emotional ties with members of the family of origin. These concepts can become manifest in unusual ways in Black families, given their traditional "connectedness" with extended and nonrelated family members.

Tom, aged 39, and Mary, aged 36, sought therapy because John, their 11-year-old son, had begun to have problems in school. Tom had worked long and hard to put himself through college and had advanced rapidly through the ranks to his position as the vice-president of a large engineering firm. He came from the "Sullivan family" and often boasted about the success of his grandfather and his father in the engineering field, although they had experienced numerous divorces and broken relationships. He rarely communicated with his father, his mother, or his grandparents, however. Furthermore, Tom maintained emotional and physical distance from his wife, their son, and their neighbors.

Mary came from a family that emphasized family togetherness. Until just before therapy, she talked three or four times per week with her mother or her grandmother about even the most routine aspects of her daily life. Tom finally complained so much about the telephone bills that Mary began to write letters in order to stay in touch with her extended family. She simultaneously moved "closer" to her son as a way of obtaining the emotional support that was no longer immediately available to her by telephone. She stopped asking Tom to accompany her on shopping or marketing trips, as he usually refused to go. Instead, she asked John to ride along, which delighted John and infuriated her husband.

Through long-term counseling, the therapist was able to help Tom and Mary understand the direct relationship between their behavior and John's current lack of success in school. Tom thought he was differentiated from his parents, but he came to understand through counseling that "cutting himself off" from his parents was simply another way of indicating strong emotional links. Mary, undifferentiated from her family of origin and extended family, could adapt to the marriage as long as her emotional system remained intact. John's difficulties in school developed when Mary began to project her emotional needs onto him. As Tom began to reestablish contact with his parents and Mary began to decrease communications with members of her family of origin and extended family, John's grades improved.

- Historically, Black men have been viewed as a major threat to a White patriarchal society. As a result, economic and social opportunities have been much more available for Black and White women than for Black men. In a society that still looks upon men as the major wage earners for their families, this not only has a demoralizing effect on the attitudes of Black men toward themselves and women, but also limits the extent to which Black men are able to be "a man" or fulfill the role of "father" (Warfield & Marion, 1985). This has also facilitated more flexible sex roles within Black American families, however, and has accounted in part for the survival of the Black family unit (Staples, 1974).

- The Black church continues to play an important role in the lives of Black families. It helps shape youngsters' attitudes toward themselves and others, allows its members to demonstrate a variety of leadership and creative talents, and often assists families in times of great distress.

> In our clinic in Newark, a family who had been seen in treatment for some time were "burned out" by a devastating fire that destroyed their home. The mother was an active member of a local Baptist church, and members of her congregation mobilized quickly to help with food, shelter, and clothing. A number of families assumed responsibility for the children for several weeks until the mother could relocate. (Hines & Boyd-Franklin, 1982, p. 96)

In addition, Black families with strong religious ties turn almost exclusively to their minister for pastoral counseling and to fellow church members for emotional support during interpersonal crises, such as child-rearing problems, divorce, suicide, death, major health problems, and the impending imprisonment of a loved one.

• The socialization of Black children is crucial for their survival and for the welfare of the entire family network. The media, particularly television, have a detrimental impact on the values, attitudes, and behavioral patterns of young people. In addition, the influence that the peer group holds over its psychologically vulnerable members increases with the decline in the number of two-parent homes. If the many social and economic barriers to full participation in society remain intact, many Black youngsters are likely to surrender to the influences of a peer group that demonstrates its hopelessness and despair through violence, substance abuse, and increased sexual promiscuity.

It is imperative for members of the Black family, especially parents and adult members of the extended family (including nonrelatives), to continue helping Black children develop racial and cultural identity in a society centered on individualism. Often, these lessons seem simple, but have serious psychological ramifications. For example, most Black parents teach their children to address individuals in positions of authority over them by an appropriate title (e.g., Mr., Mrs., Rev., Dr.). Failure to abide by this rule leads to a quick rebuke. In later life, the use of titles implies respect, structures the nature of the interaction, and indicates the manner in which the individual Black person would like to be treated.

Obstacles to Treatment

Black individuals and families are reluctant to seek professional counseling for a number of well-founded reasons. As mentioned earlier, most mental health care practitioners are White, majority culture students and professors have a decided influence on training programs, and training generally emphasizes problems experienced by middle-class White families. In addition, many theories associated with psychotherapy focus on the individual as opposed to the role of the ecosystem in determining human behavior. Being Black in America means being suspect of resources that are principally oriented toward providing services for White clientele.

Many of the attitudes implicitly, sometimes explicitly, communicated in the training of future counselors are also subtly communicated to clerical workers, secretaries, and intake workers. These staffers, who may determine if a client is seen for therapy and by whom, often reinforce the attitudes held by Blacks toward therapy.

> Mr. J. went to the local family treatment center only because his wife threatened to divorce him if he did not. He knew these "White head shrinkers" were not interested in the problems of a Black family, but he grudgingly consented to go and see "what happens." He was encouraged by the secretary who greeted the family warmly, offered them coffee, and assured them that the intake worker would be with them as soon as possible. Mr. J. was able to observe the intake worker, who was being alternately empathic with the parents and playful with the children in the White family as she made notes. As a result, he was quite unprepared for the icy stares, abrupt questions, deep sighs, and the physical distance that she maintained during her interview with his family. The intake worker, also a part-time counseling student, had learned from the supervising therapist in an informal discussion that Blacks were just too difficult to understand. Mr. J. never returned to the clinic, even though he and his family were in serious need of help.

THERAPY ISSUES WITH BLACK CLIENTS

Once Black clients have overcome their initial reluctance to engage in family therapy and have committed themselves to seeking professional help, they are likely to experience some discomfort with the techniques and procedures of counseling. Brannon (1983) pointed out that, although middle-class Blacks and Whites may have some understanding of the psychotherapeutic process, low-income Blacks may generally lack knowledge about psychotherapy. As a result, the therapist may need to educate Black family members about the realities of counseling goals and methods.

Brannon (1983) cited several differences between Black and White client systems:

- Blacks are more likely to enlist the services of a therapist in a crisis situation, because they perceive mental health care as a last resort.
- White couples tend to continue therapy for longer periods of time (e.g., 24 weekly sessions) than do Black couples (e.g., 10 sessions).
- Black clients, particularly Black men, are more guarded about themselves and more ready to discuss external issues than to communicate their intra-psychic concerns.
- Black families are more dependent on their family of origin, extended family network, and church family than is commonly appreciated by mental health care providers.

Aside from these differences, the interactions between White therapists and Black clients may be more restrained than are those between therapists and clients of the same race (Atkinson, 1983; Harrison, 1975; Sattler, 1977). As stated earlier, this may be directly associated with the dearth of training opportunities that prepare majority culture therapists for work with Black clients. Furthermore, Black clients may select a therapist with a similar racial background, preferring a helper who not only is Black, but also shares the same level of racial identification, social class, and cultural commitment (Atkinson, 1985).

FAMILY-OF-ORIGIN THERAPY WITH BLACK FAMILIES

According to Hovestadt, Anderson, Piercy, Cochran, and Fine (1985), many family practitioners have used approaches to family therapy that empha-size intergenerational influences. These strategies have obvious implications for therapy with Black families, given the significant role played by the family of origin and extended family in the day-to-day life of a Black family unit. Nonetheless, family-of-origin work with Black families must first be placed within a broad theoretical framework that adequately accounts for the unique experiences of Black people in the United States.

Gunnings and Lipscomb (1986) developed a proactive approach to work-ing with Black clients; termed *systemic counseling,* their approach is potentially of significant value if integrated with intergenerational family work. It is predicated on Pearl's (1965) theory of human behavior, which includes the assumptions:

> (a) that the individual actively interrelates with social and physical environments; (b) that the interaction is rational, is almost always conscious, is governed by self-interests, and is phenomenological in the sense that each individual has different priorities and interprets stimuli differently; (c) that the person has an active intelligence and no experience is registered without some alteration; (d) that all behavior is the consequence of a cost-benefit analysis derived from previous experience and perceived options; and (e) that all human relationships are dynamic—not only is the person influenced by environments, the human also influences environments. (Gunnings & Lipscomb, 1986, p. 18)

Gunnings and Lipscomb, thus, underscored client action and understanding systems. Their seven-step problem-solving model takes into account the social and psychological milieu of the Black client as a critical determinant in the formation of attitudes, values, and behaviors; the involvement of families of origin enhances the therapeutic process. Also, Gunnings and Lipscomb challenged the therapist to become an advocate on behalf of Black clients instead of blaming them for their inability to adjust to a racially biased and oppressive dominant culture.

Within this paradigm, it is fundamental that environmental forces, including original and extended family members, form and alter intrapsychic material. Hare and Hare (1984) provided a lucid example of the way in which "intersexual style" and values may be transmitted through generational influences in the environment when they quoted an educated Black woman married to a man who had not attended college.

> I'm not saying this right, but I think we are aggressive and dominating and domineering. But I think it's because we've had to be. Like our mothers before us and our grandmothers and great-grandmothers had to. You pick up from them. 'Cause mothers tell their daughters: You know he's not going to be able to support you, and you're going to go and have to get you an education and help him. And you know you gonna have to do this and you know you gonna have to do that. Cause you know how these men are. (Hare & Hare, 1984, p. 86)

In view of this intergenerationally triggered attitude toward Black men, it is little wonder that Black relationships are plagued by communication difficulties, inappropriate perceptions of self, and the devaluation of opposite gender roles within the Black family (Brannon, 1983).

The effectiveness of family-of-origin work with Black families is predicated on several essential assumptions. Initially, the therapist must make a deliberate effort to gain the trust of Black clients. As indicated earlier, this may be difficult. Furthermore, the level of trust and the level of disclosure with Black families are likely to fluctuate based on the issues being discussed and length of time in therapy.

In the first few sessions of therapy, it is best to glean an understanding of the problem, learn about extended and nonrelated family members, note social systems that affect the difficulty, establish a structure for counseling (e.g., family members each speak for themselves and avoid derogatory remarks), and communicate expectations for the family members who are attending, as well as for those who may join the sessions at a later date. Instruments such as the *Personal Authority in the Family System Questionnaire* (Bray, Williamson, & Malone, 1984) and the *Family of Origin Scale* (Hovestadt et al., 1985) can be effective tools in orienting Black family members to family-of-origin sessions, once the initial crises have been appropriately managed; however, it may be necessary to bring in members of the family of origin to help resolve the initial crises.

Many Black families are much more willing to include members of the family of origin in counseling sessions than are White families. This may be because they want to correct a problem immediately or because they generally remain in close touch with a large number of relatives.

> In an early therapy session with a single Black mother and her child, the mother repeatedly urged the therapist to call her mother, the child's maternal grandmother, to confirm the similarities between her mother's child-rearing practices and her own. After two three-way telephone conversations, the client seemed much more relaxed and less resistant to therapy.

Clearly, therapists must be flexible and creative in their attempts to employ family-of-origin techniques with Black clients. Physical handicaps, financial constraints, and transportation problems may require unusual strategies to involve members of the family of origin.

In the process of family-of-origin therapy with Black families, it is helpful to identify specific unresolved family-of-origin issues that affect the current problem. Sometimes, in order to do so, it is necessary to obtain information from a parent or an agency in the period between weekly sessions. For example, in the case of Tom, Mary, and John, the therapist asked the parents to find out before the second session exactly when John first began doing poorly in school.

Concurrent with the establishment of some degree of trust and subsequent to the resolution of some of the initial specified family-of-origin issues, the family is often more receptive to therapeutic confrontation, cajoling, leveling, and self-disclosing from the therapist. In a similar fashion, the therapist may use written contracts, role-playing techniques, audiotapes to be played at home, listening and communication exercises, paradoxes, reframing the problem, and direct instructional activities to help family members move toward a higher level of functioning.

The therapist should focus on cementing changes in the ways that family members relate to each other and ensuring that they carry with them a model to use for solving other problems as they arise. As therapy progresses, the clients should assume more responsibility for the content of the sessions. For example, the therapist may encourage them to summarize or highlight individual sessions and let them assume a more prominent role in determining homework assignments.

CONCLUSION

Effective work with Black families requires mental health care practitioners to develop an enhanced understanding of the dynamics that have helped to shape these family units. Recognition of the severe limitations of current counseling approaches as applied to Black clients is paramount. As culturally sensitive therapists seek to facilitate change in the dynamics of Black families, they must significantly modify old approaches and rely on more innovative theories that give credence to the role of the ecosystem in shaping and ameliorating family problems. Advocacy, flexibility, and change should be the tools of the family therapist who works with Black clients.

REFERENCES

Atkinson, D.R. (1983). Ethnic similarity in counseling psychology: A review of research. *The Counseling Psychologist, 11*(3), 79–92.

Atkinson, D.R. (1985). A meta-review of research on cross-cultural counseling and psychotherapy. *Journal of Multicultural Counseling and Development, 13*(1), 138–153.

Bowen, M. (1978). *Family therapy in clinical practice.* New York: Jason Aronson.

Brannon, L. (1983). Marriage and family therapy with Black clients: Method and structure. In C. Obudho (Ed.), *Black marriage and family therapy* (pp. 169–188). Westport, CT: Greenwood Press.

Bray, J.H., Williamson, D.S., & Malone. P.E. (1984). Personal authority in the family system: Development of a questionnaire to measure personal authority in intergenerational family processes. *Journal of Marital and Family Therapy, 10*(2), 167–178.

Framo, J.L. (1981). The integration of marital therapy with sessions with family of origin. In A. Gurman & D. Kinskern (Eds.), *Handbook of family therapy* (pp. 133–158). New York: Brunner/Mazel.

Gunnings, T.S., & Lipscomb, W.D. (1986). Psychotherapy for Black men: A systemic approach. *Journal of Multicultural Counseling and Development, 14*(1), 17–24.

Hare, N., & Hare, J. (1984). *The endangered Black family: Coping with the unisexualization and the coming extinction of the Black race.* San Francisco: Black Think Tank.

Harrison, D.K. (1975). Race as a counselor-client variable in counseling and psychotherapy: A review of the research. *The Counseling Psychologist, 5*(1), 124–133.

Hines, P., & Boyd-Franklin, N. (1982). Black families. In M. McGoldrick, J. Pearce, & J. Giordano (Eds.), *Ethnicity and family therapy* (pp. 84–107). New York: Guilford Press.

Hovestadt, A.J., Anderson, W.T., Piercy, F.P., Cochran, S.W., & Fine, M. (1985). A family of origin scale. *Journal of Marital and Family Therapy, 11*(3), 287–297.

McAdoo, H. (1977). Family therapy in the Black community. *American Journal of Orthopsychiatry, 47*(1), 75–79.

Nobles, W. (1974). Africanity: Its role in Black families. *The Black Scholar, 5*(9), 10–17.

Pearl, A. (1965). *Psychology and mental health.* Santa Cruz: University of California, Santa Cruz.

Sattler, J.M. (1977). The effects of therapist-client racial similarity. In A.S. Gurman & A.M. Razin (Eds.), *Effective psychotherapy: A handbook of research* (pp. 252–290). New York: Pergamon Press.

Staples, R. (1974). The Black family in evolutionary perspective. *The Black Scholar, 5*(9), 2–9.

U.S. Bureau of the Census. (1986). *We, the Black Americans* (Report #3). Washington, DC: U.S. Government Printing Office.

Warfield, J., & Marion, R. (1985). Counseling the Black male. *Journal of Non-White Concerns in Personnel and Guidance, 13*(2), 54–71.

8. Family-of-Origin Work in Training and Supervision

Milo F. Benningfield, PhD
Psychologist, Private Practice
Faculty, Southwest Family Institute
Dallas, Texas

In spite of a proliferation of articles, a few books, and a significant number of presentations on the training and supervision of family therapists (Liddle, 1985/86), the most effective approach—or approaches—for training and supervising family therapists has yet to be determined. Until there is a standard body of knowledge, including agreed upon goals and treatment modalities, the debate regarding the relative efficacy of the predominant models of family therapy supervision seems likely to continue. As Beavers (1985/86) observed, "At present, family therapy supervision is a potpourri of many varied theoretical underpinnings" (p. 15). It seems premature to determine which of the various training formats and philosophies should remain and which should be eliminated. According to Ganahl, Ferguson, and L'Abate, (1985), it is necessary first to examine the benefits of each and consider how each might be effectively integrated into a single approach.

One training/supervision model that is currently receiving attention focuses on the influence of the trainee's family of origin on the trainee's therapeutic style and development. Supervisors who use a multigenerational approach with client families encourage trainees to do likewise with their own families (Bowen, 1978; Kramer, 1985; Williamson, 1981b). Indeed, supervisors who emphasize the personal growth of the trainee believe such a focus to be important, if not imperative. Skynner (1981) maintained that skill training is of little value without a concomitant emphasis on the personal growth of the therapist. Framo (1982) noted that each therapist should examine his own "gut issues of family life which have been burned indelibly into his mind" (p. 276).

HISTORY

The first direct application of family-of-origin work to the training and supervision of family therapists is credited to Murray Bowen. Like so many innovations in the family therapy field, it occurred serendipitously (Bowen, 1978). After several months of examining the emotional forces, triangles, and relational interactions in his family of origin, Bowen decided to see if he could interact with the members of his family in a more differentiated manner, thus putting into practice what he had been preaching and teaching psychiatric residents to do for some years. His primary goal was to avoid entanglement in his family's emotional force field and yet to interact with each family member in a more personal and meaningful manner. This success of this experiment had a profound influence on Bowen, both personally and professionally.

In 1967, at a family therapy conference in Philadelphia, Bowen shared this very personal experience with his professional colleagues. Then he began sharing aspects of his experience with his students, relating it to families in general. His students, in turn, began to use similar strategies with their own parents and siblings, reporting some success. Since that time, hundreds of therapists have studied with Bowen in order to learn how to apply this approach to their own lives, as well as to those of their trainees and clients (Simon, 1980).

While Bowen was encouraging students to work on unfinished family-of-origin issues through face-to-face contact with their parents and siblings, Virginia Satir was using a group format to help students work through unfinished business with their families of origin. Members of the group acted out multi-generational themes in order to go "back to old situations with new eyes" (Nerin, 1986, p. viii). This approach has come to be known as family reconstruction.

Meanwhile, James Framo was having trainees write family biographies and/or bring their families into the class for family consultations in order to resolve continuing issues with their parents, siblings, and grandparents. In addition, he shared his own experiences in conducting family-of-origin sessions with clients (Framo, 1982).

By the mid-1970s, increasing numbers of family therapists were alerting trainees to the possibility that unresolved issues with their families of origin might interfere with their personal and professional growth as therapists. Family therapy educators and supervisors were beginning to use a combination of home visits, family reconstruction techniques, and office consultations with both clients and trainees (Kramer, 1985; Nerin, 1986; Paul & Paul, 1975; Williamson, 1982). By the turn of the century, family-of-origin work will probably be integrated into most of the major approaches to family therapy, training, and supervision (Berger, 1982; Forman, 1984; Hatcher, 1978).

RATIONALE

The reasons for encouraging trainees to focus on their own families of origin are all intimately related to the eventual effectiveness of their work with client families. For example, therapists who have worked through unfinished business with their parents, grandparents, and siblings do not feel threatened or intimidated by older clients. They have no need to invest time and energy in seeking acceptance or approval from client families, because they have established their personal beliefs and position in their original family (Carter & Orfanidis, 1976); they do not use client families to work out unfinished business in their own family. Their ability to individuate within their original family contributes to an emotional and intellectual maturity that, in turn, increases their capacity to work with client families without becoming entangled in the emotional or psychological field of these families (Kerr, 1984). Finally, when therapists can move in and out of their family of origin comfortably, their own family can become a valuable resource in their work with client families (Williamson, 1981a). Indeed, understanding makes their own family of origin an ally rather than an adversary as therapists work with clients.

People tend to reenact their early family behaviors in their subsequent significant relationships. Thus, trainees are likely to repeat the interpersonal patterns of behavior that they learned in their original family with client families, particularly with families that generate anxieties and tensions similar to those experienced in the original family. An awareness of such patterns and an understanding of the ways in which those patterns tend to be activated in therapy enable the therapist to monitor them effectively and replace them with more therapeutic ones (Protinsky & Keller, 1984). The trainee who is aware of the complexity of family-of-origin relationships and the challenge of learning to interact in more positive, mature ways does not have simplistic and narrow notions about the reasons for clients' behavior and the slowness with which constructive change occurs.

People develop their sense of self and their interpersonal skills within their families of origin. Failure to explore the family of origin in training removes a valuable learning resource. The opportunity for trainees to examine their original family from a historical perspective enhances their ability to correct emotional and perceptual distortions, which, in turn, facilitates more objective and therapeutic interaction with client families (Braverman, 1982; Kramer, 1985). Examining the dynamics at work in their own family of origin helps trainees to understand and appreciate the powerful forces that operate in client families under stress. As Kramer (1985) explained, just as client families bring into the consultation room their own unique experiences and learnings from the past, so do therapists.

Many problems thought to be technical in nature are actually relationship issues, and simply obtaining more technical information is not likely to correct such problems (Kramer, 1980). The intensity of family interaction in the consultation room can quickly amplify such feelings as helplessness, anger, or disgust in the therapist. These feelings can thwart the therapist's ability to work effectively with the family, regardless of the extent of the therapist's technical skills. For example, trainees may use their family of origin as the standard against which they determine the degree of health or illness in client families. If, as Kramer (1980) explained, trainees view their family of origin as healthy, they may overlook or minimize dysfunctional patterns in a client family that resembles their family of origin. On the other hand, if the client family differs considerably from their "normal" family, the trainees may misdiagnose this difference as pathology. Again, client families stimulate their therapist to reflect on early family-of-origin relationships, and these relationships significantly influence the manner in which therapists relate to client families in the present—despite their technical training.

GOALS

The ultimate goal of focusing on a trainee's family of origin is to increase the trainee's later effectiveness as a therapist. Therefore, the goals of family-of-origin work with trainees include

- preventing nontherapeutic triangulation
- preventing the use of client families to resolve unfinished business in the trainee's family of origin
- identifying and attending to mythological beliefs about the trainee's family of origin, as well as client families
- minimizing the influence of dysfunctional transgenerational issues in the therapy session
- helping the trainee to claim, and exercise appropriately, personal power and authority as a therapist

Trainees who understand that triangles are inevitable when family members are caught up in sustained conflict can use this information therapeutically. If the trainees have already dealt with this issue successfully in their family of origin, they are more likely to handle it successfully in client families. It is common for a family therapy trainee to side with one family member, especially when tension and anxiety are high in the consultation room and the trainee was in a similar family-of-origin relationship as a child or adolescent.

> A seasoned, individually trained therapist found himself consistently joining with wives against their forceful husbands. In exploring his behavior as a youth, he realized that he had behaved similarly toward his mother in an effort to "protect her from my domineering father." His recognition of this pattern, combined with some personal dialogue with each of his parents, enabled him to approach client couples in a more balanced, therapeutic manner. Furthermore, he was subsequently better able to move in and out of client families without becoming excessively involved or distant with any of the family members.

Family therapists often come into the profession with unresolved conflicts and issues with parents, siblings, and other relatives. Frequently, such information is out of the trainee's conscious awareness or, at best, minimized (Framo, 1982). Recognizing and attending to these unresolved family-of-origin issues lessen the likelihood that the therapist will activate them with client families in unproductive, nontherapeutic ways.

A family myth is a belief about the family that is shared by all its members. Generally, such a myth goes unchallenged and contributes to the shape of family roles and interactions, despite the fact that it may be an exaggeration or a distortion of reality (Sauber, L'Abate, & Weeks, 1985).

> A trainee found herself consistently stalled with families who operated under the myth that conflicts or disagreements are always destructive. A similar myth operated in her own family of origin, and she had faithfully abided by it and perpetuated it, even into adulthood. By directly addressing this myth in her family of origin, she learned to address it therapeutically in client families.

Like everyone else, family therapists come from less than perfect families. Thus, they usually learn some patterns of communication and interaction in their childhood and adolescence that are counterproductive to optimal growth and development as a family therapist. One trainee explained it this way: "As I have become less anxious and protective about my own toxic issues, I have been more effective at opening up, listening to and helping families deal with their own 'hot spots' " (Anonymous, 1979, p. 76). It is not stress or turmoil that causes a therapist to become entangled in families, but rather the therapist's reaction to the stress or turmoil. By controlling personal reactions to emotionally charged situations, a therapist can diminish personal anxiety, which, in turn, can have a calming influence on the client family.

Even the most seasoned of family therapists can become entangled in a client family's emotional field. In order to avoid being drawn into a client family's demands and persuasions, trainees must be clear and comfortable with their convictions and actions as adults. As Williamson (1982) emphasized, therapists must be able to exercise personal authority with clients in order not to be intimidated by older or younger generations.

> A 39-year-old psychologist began to cry when her mother comfortably accepted her request to address her by her first name. "I guess," she reflected, "if I give up calling you Mother, I will have to give up being your little girl." It was a major challenge for this psychologist to claim and exercise the competent adult part of herself and to give up the wish for client families to respond positively to the sweet little girl part of herself.

According to Keen (1970), as long as people stay with the authority models that gave shape to their existence in the past, they remain children living in a world of adults who have exceeding power over one's life.

APPLICATIONS

A family-of-origin training/supervision experience that integrates cognitive information, skill training, and experiential opportunities introduces trainees to the major therapeutic family therapy models and techniques associated with them.

> Samuel, a doctoral student in a family therapy program, consistently aligned himself in an overprotective manner with the mothers and remained distant and aloof from the fathers in the families with which he worked. Despite feedback from his supervisor and group members, Samuel insisted that the type of families assigned to him determined his particular style of relating to the parents. It had nothing to do with him personally.
>
> Following two sessions of the supervision group in which the participants examined and shared the personal impact of a death in their families, Samuel visited his father's grave for the first time since his father's death when Samuel was 6 years of age. With

group support and encouragement, this 42-year-old man eventually made several visits to his father's grave and recorded "conversations" with his father that he later shared with the training group. It was a very powerful experience for the group to hear Samuel recall at the gravesite a long forgotten memory. Shortly before his death, Samuel's father had said, "Samuel, promise me that you will take very good care of females always—especially your mother and sisters."

On a subsequent visit to his father's grave, Samuel recorded, "Dad, you asked too much of that 6-year-old child when you insisted he take special care of females for the rest of his life, even though I tried desperately to fulfill that command for the past 36 years. It has not only been an impossible task and burden, but it has interfered with my being comfortable and close to men."

Dealing with repressed memories and unresolved grief related to his father's death eventually enabled Samuel to relate to couples and parents in therapy in a more balanced, unbiased manner (see Paul, 1983; Williamson, 1978).

Patrick had little tolerance for wives who had multiple complaints and acted weak or needy in sessions. He tended to lecture them and to withhold empathy and support.

When Patrick was 8 years old, his parents divorced. Patrick and his siblings remained with their father. Their mother moved several hundred miles away and had virtually no contact with them from that time forward. When Patrick asked why his mother never wrote or called, his father responded, "Your mother is not emotionally well and has too little energy for doing much."

One afternoon in the family-of-origin group, Patrick thought out loud, "I wonder if my impatience with seemingly needy females has anything to do with my own mother?" During the following Spring break, Patrick visited the home of his mother and her aging parents—not having seen any of them for the past 26 years. Listening to his mother describe her shame and pain regarding her hospitalization for psychiatric care shortly after her divorce from his father and her belief that her children could never forgive her for "leaving them," Patrick began to perceive his mother as a human being who had strengths and weaknesses, fears and regrets, just as most other people have. He also discovered during this and subsequent visits with his mother that he himself had many of her positive attributes and qualities.

At the conclusion of the 2-year training program, Patrick wrote on his evaluation form: "The personal existential experience with my mother last spring, in addition to subsequent contact with her, not only helped me to grow personally but helped me appreciate and work more effectively with needy, dependent clients— especially female clients!"

With clients who seemed very competent and self-assured, Sandra tended to use a high-pitched, compliant, little girl voice. She explained that she felt like a little girl with many families, especially those in which the parents were considerably older than she. She added that, although she was 36 years old, married, and the mother of two teen-agers, she still felt like a "little girl" in her family of origin.

Shortly before one of her periodic visits to her parents' home, Sandra asked the supervision group to suggest things she might do to "feel more adult" in the presence of her parents. Following a detailed description of a typical weekend with her parents when she visited them alone, the supervisor and the group members made several suggestions. For example, they advised Sandra to ask her father to carry her luggage out of the airport instead of engaging with him in a tug of war over this issue. When they reached the car, Sandra was to open the back door for her mother and usher her in; Sandra was to sit in the front seat where she could talk more easily with both parents, rather than in the back seat as she usually did. Furthermore, Sandra was instructed to pick a restaurant where she wanted to eat, instead of saying her usual "It doesn't matter," and explain to her parents that she would go with them only if it was agreed that she would pick up the check.

Armed with a few additional "strategies," Sandra flew to her parents' home for a few days. When she returned, she described the visit as one of the best she had "ever had with my mother and dad." Nearly a year later, Sandra credited these visits as largely responsible for her ability to take a much more active role with couples and families, to speak with an authoritative adult voice, and to feel comfortable giving regular out-of-session assignments to clients.

John had a tendency to overidentify with clients who were the younger members of the families with which he worked. In addition, he regularly opposed the mothers and was overly protective with the fathers.

Following one particularly agonizing family therapy session in which John completely lost his temper, yelled furiously at the mother, and told the father and the teen-agers in the family that they had an "impossible wife and mother with whom one could not get in a word edgewise," John sought help from his supervision group. They encouraged John to visit his parents on a holiday when his siblings would be there, to observe the typical patterns of interaction and communication among family members, and to tape several conversations with family members, both individually and together. As John played portions of the tapes for the supervision group a few days after his visit, he was stunned at the similarities between the communication style of his family of origin and that of client families with which he had difficulties. At one point, he blurted out, "My mother and I sound just like the mother and me on the tape I shared with the group the other day!"

Following this session, John scheduled a series of visits with each member of his family to work on becoming less reactive emotionally within his family, which, in turn, enabled him to be less reactive with client families.

CONCLUSION

Asking family therapy trainees to examine and deal with the dynamics of their own families of origin is much more than an academic exercise. It is a rigorous, demanding process. Increasing numbers of family therapy educators and supervisors are requiring their trainees to perform such a task, however, because they believe that it is not only helpful and informative for the trainees, but also essential to their development as effective family therapists. Examining their own family of origin facilitates trainees' inventiveness and creativity with clients. It also encourages an integrative approach to family treatment. Perhaps most significantly, it helps to minimize the trainee's proclivity to repeat early, unproductive family patterns with client families or to use client families to resolve their unfinished family-of-origin issues.

REFERENCES

Anonymous. (1979). My trip into separateness and connectedness. *The Family, 6*(2), 72–76.

Beavers, R.W. (1985/86). Family therapy supervision: An introduction and consumer's guide. *Journal of Psychotherapy and the Family, 1,* 15–24.

Berger, M. (1982). The strategic use of "Bowenian" formulations. *The Journal of Strategic and Systemic Therapies, 1*(4), 50–56.

Bowen, M. (1978). *Family therapy in clinical practice.* New York: Jason Aronson.

Braverman, S. (1982). Family of origin as a training resource for family therapists. *Canadian Journal of Psychiatry, 27,* 629–633.

Carter, E.A., & Orfanidis, M. (1976). Family therapy with one person and the family therapist's own family. In P. Guerin (Ed.), *Family therapy* (pp. 193–219). New York: Gardner Press.

Forman, B. (1984). Family of origin work in systemic/strategic therapy training. In. C.E. Munson (Ed.), *Family of origin applications in clinical supervision* (pp. 81–85). New York: Haworth Press.

Framo, J. (1982). *Explorations in marital and family therapy: Selected papers of James L. Framo.* New York: Springer.

Ganahl, G., Ferguson, L., & L'Abate, L. (1985). In L. L'Abate (Ed.), *The handbook of family psychology and therapy* (pp. 1281–1317). Homewood, IL: Dorsay Press.

Hatcher, C. (1978). Intrapersonal and interpersonal models: Blending Gestalt and family therapies. *Journal of Marriage and Family Counseling, 4,* 63–68.

Keen, S. (1970). *To a dancing god.* New York: Harper & Row.

Kerr, M.E. (1984). Theoretical base for differentiation of self in one's family of origin. In C.E. Munson (Ed.), *Family of origin applications in clinical supervision* (pp. 3–36). New York: Haworth Press.

Kramer, C. (1980). *Becoming a family therapist.* New York: Human Sciences Press.

Kramer, J.R. (1985). *Family interfaces: Transgenerational patterns.* New York: Brunner/Mazel.

Liddle, H. (1985/86). Redefining the mission of family therapy training: Can our differences make a difference? *Journal of Psychotherapy and the Family, 1,* 109–124.

Nerin, W.F. (1986). *Family reconstruction: Long day's journey into light.* New York: W.W. Norton.

Paul, N. (1983). The unconscious transmission of hidden images and the schizophrenic process. In H. Stierlin, L.C. Wynne, & M. Wirsching (Eds.), *Psychosocial intervention in schizophrenia: An international view* (pp. 199–213). New York: Springer, Verlag.

Paul, N., & Paul, B. (1975). *A marital puzzle.* New York: W.W. Norton.

Protinsky, H., & Keller, J. (1984). Supervision of marriage and family therapy: A family of origin approach. In C.E. Munson (Ed.), *Family of origin applications in clinical supervision* (pp. 75–80). New York: Haworth Press.

Sauber, S.R., L'Abate, L., & Weeks, G. (1985). *Family therapy: Basic concepts and terms.* Rockville, MD: Aspen Publishers.

Simon, R. (1980). A network geneology: A history of family therapy in the Baltimore-Washington corridor, *Family therapy practice network newsletter, 4*(1), 1–10.

Skynner, A.C.R. (1981). An open-systems, group-analytic approach to family therapy. In A. Gurman & D. Kniskern (Eds.), *Handbook of family therapy* (pp. 39–84). New York: Brunner/Mazel.

Williamson, D. (1978). New life at the graveyard: A method of therapy for individuation from a dead former parent. *Journal of Marriage and Family Counseling, 7*(4), 93–101.

Williamson, D. (1981a). Debriefing the past president. *AAMFT Newsletter, 12*(2), 9.

Williamson, D. (1981b). Termination of the intergenerational hierarchical boundary between the first and second generations: A new stage in the family life cycle. *Journal of Marital and Family Therapy, 7,* 441–453.

Williamson, D. (1982). Personal authority via termination of the intergenerational hierarchical boundary: Part II. The consultation process and the therapeutic method. *Journal of Marital and Family Therapy, 8,* 23–37.

9. An Academic Course on Family-of-Origin Issues

William T. Anderson, EdD
Lecturer ad Interim
Family and Consumer Studies
Texas Woman's University
Denton, Texas

Relatively few people are aware of how they continue to be influenced and controlled in their behavior by the unachieved goals and the unresolved problems of the parental and the grandparental generations. (Williamson, 1978, p. 94)

Many graduate training programs in marriage and family counseling require students to participate in group processes or group therapy as part of their preparation for working with couples and families. Yet, it seems more relevant for therapists to deal with relationships in their own family of origin than with relationships among fellow graduate students. The shared experience with fellow graduate students over one semester can be helpful; more helpful and more enduring, however, is students' work on their family of origin, a personal system that therapists regularly take with them into their counseling sessions. Thus, the rationale for requiring students to work on family-of-origin issues is the same as that applied by Framo (1981) to his work with groups of three couples in family-of-origin therapy. He explained that he focused on each couple, "rather than the group because that pair had a history before the group started and is likely to have a future together long after the group is disbanded" (p. 148).

One way to help students of family therapy work on their own family-of-origin issues is to offer a formal, academic graduate course on such issues. This article contains practical course suggestions that have been derived from experience.

COURSE OBJECTIVES

A formal course in family-of-origin issues has three objectives:

1. an adequate understanding of the theoretical bases for family-of-origin work
2. knowledge of selected techniques that student therapists can use in family-of-origin therapy
3. personal work by students in dealing with important issues in their own families of origin

The emphasis is on the students' relationships with *their own families,* not with other graduates. This course is, thus, partially didactic, partially experiential.

At the beginning of the course, the teacher informs students of the three objectives and asks them to keep confidential the personal experiences that are shared in class. Students' working on their family of origin in an academic situation brings up such important issues as their trust in the teacher and in other class members, their willingness to do such work in the classroom atmosphere, and the importance of dealing with any problems that may arise from the approach (Braverman, 1982). Walking the fine line between an academic experience and a therapy group is a challenge to the teacher that is well worth the effort.

COURSE FORMAT

Two texts are used for the course: *Making Peace with Your Parents* by Harold Bloomfield (1983) and *Genograms in Family Assessment* by McGoldrick and Gerson (1985). Bloomfield's book provides fertile material for student reaction papers; McGoldrick and Gerson provide an excellent introduction to the use of the genogram in family-of-origin work.

COURSE PROGRESSION

Beginning Phase

The first class session in the family-of-origin course is similar in many ways to other purely academic courses. Students arrive, wondering what the professor is like, how much effort he will require, and how difficult it will be to get an A! This course, however, has an added dimension: work on one's own family of origin, both during the class and through homework assignments. The students seem both anxious and eager, wondering where this professor will lead them, yet somewhat impatient to begin the journey.

The author has found it helpful during the first class session to make very clear the 3 basic objectives of the course. Especially helpful is a clear explanation of some specific assignments in the students' personal work with their own families of origin. Already during the first class session, the professor can "hear" some of the students' questions: How far can I trust this teacher? Do I really want to share my personal familial relationships with these other students, many of whom are strangers to me? Will I be *required* to reveal my family secrets, even if I am not ready or willing to do so? If a student is overwhelmed emotionally, is the professor prepared to handle such a possibility? Most of all, do I trust myself enough to embark on this long journey? Am I able and should I go home again to my family of origin?

The genogram of the professor's own family of origin is a good place to begin. If the teacher illustrates this technique during the first or second class session, students experience this self-disclosure as a gentle invitation to begin their own journey. This approach encourages many students to commence their own family-of-origin trip. Regular readings and reaction papers from Bloomfield (1985) also help students look at relevant emotional issues rooted in their family-of-origin relationships.

This initial phase of the course includes lectures on the theoretical bases of family-of-origin work. A good starting place is the Bowenian model of family systems (Bowen, 1978). His stress on autonomy and differentiation de-emphasizing the emotional aspects of family relationships provides the student with a safe, intellectual point of departure for the family-of-origin journey. Intimacy issues can come later!

Middle Phase

Each week, subtle but important changes occur in the class, much like a young shoot sprouting from the soil. The weekly lecture, the regular reaction papers, the student presentations, the teacher's competence and trust, and especially the sharing in the small groups: all these serve to foster growth, trust, and openness in the class members.

During this middle phase, work in class focuses on the family life cycle, family-of-origin patterns, transgenerational myths and rules, sibling systems, and present adult relationships (sibling, spousal, and friendship). Students are encouraged to critique theoretical paradigms, especially in light of their own past and present family-of-origin relationships. This is a good time to introduce the object relations approach of Fairbairn, Dicks, Boszormenyi-Nagy, and Framo.

Most students have by now begun their journey, becoming more aware of the powerful emotions embedded in themselves and in their family-of-origin system. Many students begin to deal with powerful repressed feelings rooted in family violence, incest, neglect, emotional cut-offs, family secrets, unresolved grief, and a growing desire among family members to return to their roots, to relate to one another as human beings, and to face squarely the aging and ultimate death of each member—first their parents and then themselves.

Sharing these emotions when and if they wish, the students gradually develop a closeness that is quite different from that of an interpersonal process course. Here, the emphasis remains on one's own family of origin; fellow students become supportive allies, since they, too, are dealing with unresolved issues in their own family of origin. In the small groups, students regularly facilitate the efforts of one another to become separate and close at the same time with significant members in the family of origin.

Concluding Phase

As the course nears completion, students complete their work on an integrative paper. Many students are now more open, less defensive, and more "differentiated," not only with their own family of origin, but also with one another and with the teacher.

During this final phase of the course, one can introduce the students to Williamson's "new stage in the family life cycle" (1981), as well as to the existential views of Carl Whitaker (Whitaker and Keith, 1981) and to the systemic family-of-origin work with couples done by Beavers (1985).

TEACHING TECHNIQUES

Theoretical Background

Each class period, the teacher presents an aspect of the theory on which family-of-origin work is based. In addition, students are required to read selected chapters from Bowen (1978), Boszormenyi-Nagy and Ulrich (1981), Framo (1976, 1981), Napier and Whitaker (1978), Whitaker and Keith (1981), and Williamson (1981, 1982a, 1982b) and show their understanding of these "classics" through term papers or written examinations. They are encouraged to wrestle with the concepts presented and to apply them to their own experiences, either in their own family of origin or in their work with couples and families.

Students also present class reports on relevant research from recent professional journals. The bibliographies found in McGoldrick and Gerson (1985) and Kramer (1985) provide many journal articles related to family-of-origin work. Once again, the teacher encourages the class to critique the hypotheses, the limitations, the design, and the conclusions of the studies.

Reaction Papers

Regularly, students prepare two-page, double-spaced reaction papers focused on a specific issue. For example, after reading "Dealing with Parental Aging, Dying, and Death" (Bloomfield, 1983, chapter 6) students write on the following topic: "How I Am Preparing for the Death of My Parent(s)." Similar reaction papers deal with mother, father, sexual messages, siblings, resentment and anger, autonomy, closeness, and traumas. The reaction papers focus on the students' own profound feelings, experiences, beliefs, and internalized values in regard to these topics, much of which is rooted in their own families of origin.

The teacher reads each paper and returns them with written comments; these papers are not shared directly with the class. The depth and the power of many of these reaction papers is astonishing, as students at different levels and at different rhythms begin to face "the unachieved goals and the unresolved problems" (Williamson, 1978, p. 94) from their childhood that continue to affect them. Some students experienced the professor's comments, written in *red*, as "parental corrections!" Changing the pen color was easy; more difficult was identifying and dealing with the instinctive reactions to authority figures (myths), first experienced in the parents, and now experienced by the professor!

Small Groups

Groups of four or five students meet together throughout the course at least once each class period to discuss relevant topics and share feelings. Often, the topic assigned is the same as the topic assigned for the most recently completed reaction paper. These small group sessions focus on the work that students are doing with their own family of origin, not with their interpersonal relationships with the other students. The depth of discussion seems to vary widely, depending on the individual students, the level of trust in the group, and the specific topic being discussed.

I once tried to facilitate a class discussion on sexual messages in the family of origin; the class responded with a deafening silence, a tribute to the affective component of such a topic. The next week, I presented each group with clinical cases that dealt with the same sexual issues. This time, the groups relaxed, the discussion became animated, and the family-of-origin "tapes" came rolling out! The third week, the class processed the contrast between these two experiences.

Rules and Rituals

Studies dealing with family rules (Ford, 1983) and family rituals (Wolin & Bennett, 1984) provide additional lecture material. To make this more relevant, the teacher can construct simple checklists of rules and rituals. Students can check the rules and rituals both in their own family of origin and in their present adult relationships. These checklists become the focus of discussion and sharing in the small groups, as the students note similarities and differences between the rules and rituals in the family of origin and those in present relationships. This teaching technique can also be used with other aspects of the family of origin.

The Genogram

The literature on the genogram and its use in family-of-origin work is extensive (e.g., Bradt, 1980; Duhl, Kantor, & Duhl, 1973; Guerin & Pendagast, 1976; Hof & Berman, 1986; Jolly, Froom, & Rosen, 1980; Lieberman, 1979; McGoldrick & Gerson, 1985; Wachtel, 1982). One effective way to introduce the genogram in class is to have one student interview the teacher to illustrate how to construct a genogram with a client.

Using McGoldrick and Gerson's clear explanation (1985), the students begin their own family genogram. Students then share their genograms in dyads, in their regular groups, or with the entire class. They learn to collect factual information first, beginning in the sibling generation and ending with the grandparental generation. Then they gather relationship information (e.g., triangles, rules, binds, myths), beginning with the grandparental generation and ending with the sibling generation.

This personal genogram makes students consciously aware of important aspects of the family system into which they were born. As they begin to make contacts (e.g., personal visits, telephone calls, letters) with various members of their extended family, students regularly report in class about family secrets discovered, about triangles previously recognized only vaguely, and about family rules and myths passed down through generations. Students become aware, some for the first time, of various healthy aspects of their family. This work on the genogram often helps students to reestablish emotional connections, to understand the family from their parents' perspective, and to place themselves in the family system through time: first as children, then adults, and eventually grandparents.

Family Photographs

Anderson and Malloy (1976) noted that family photographs can be used effectively in therapy. This same technique can be employed in a graduate course. The teacher asks students to bring to class three photographs from their childhood to illustrate those family relationships that they consider important. The relationships shown in the photographs can be discussed in dyads, the regular groups, or even with the entire class. The photographs often reveal to other students what is not so evident to the student involved. This indirect way of dealing with family relationships has frequently helped reluctant students talk about relationships in their family of origin.

Family Sculpting

Kramer (1985) aptly noted that family sculpting is "to experience an alternate language composed of space and action expressed both nonverbally and verbally" (p. 110). Her discussion provides ample material for an explanation of the use of family sculpting in family-of-origin work. Other excellent sources of ideas are found in Constantine (1978); Jefferson (1978); Papp, Silverstein, and Carter (1973); and Simon (1972).

A Family Myth Experience

When one class was discussing family myths, a creative student suggested to the teacher, unknown to the rest of the students, a class "experience." Normally, students were allotted 10 minutes to present their critique of a journal article. As she had suggested, the teacher allowed this student only 5 minutes, a fact obvious to all the other students. Later in that class period, the student confronted the teacher about his mistake regarding her time. The increased level of anxiety in the class became quickly apparent to everyone. Once this happened, the student proceeded to discuss the experience. What myths about confronting authority (parents) were activated? What "disasters" did the other students expect to befall the confronting student? Clearly, the childhood patterns of relating to authority (older generation) had reappeared in the class of adults.

Self-Disclosure

Perhaps one of the most powerful teaching techniques for a course in family-of-origin issues is the teacher's appropriate self-disclosure. In therapy, self-disclosure is usually helpful when it relates to a client's present concerns and when it enables the client to deal more effectively with his or her own issues. In the classroom, the teacher's appropriate self-disclosure may motivate students to examine their own family roots.

Family-of-Origin Scales

In the field of family-of-origin therapy, theoretical concepts and applied clinical work seem to be more highly developed than are scales and questionnaires. Two instruments have been published, however, that are useful not only in clinical practice, but also in a graduate class.

The *Family of Origin Scale* (Hovestadt, Anderson, Piercy, Cochran, & Fine, 1985) is designed to measure perceived levels of health in the family of origin. Rooted in the health model described by Lewis, Beavers, Gosset, and Phillips (1976), this scale is built on the two axes of autonomy and intimacy, major elements of individual and family health. It is simple to administer and to score; the *Family of Origin Scale* easily generates class discussion about key concepts in individual and family health.

The *Personal Authority in the Family System Questionnaire* (Bray, Williamson, & Malone, 1984) is designed to measure an adult's personal authority (Williamson, 1981, 1982a, 1982b) in three generations: (1) parents, (2) spouse, and (3) children. In contrast to the *Family of Origin Scale,* the *Personal Authority in the Family System Questionnaire* focuses on *present* relationships, not perceptions of past levels of family health.

An Integrative Paper

Near the end of the course, the teacher can assign a final paper in which the students synthesize and integrate what they have learned about their family of origin. Such a paper may cover such areas as the family genogram, the student's personal perceptions of both parents and siblings, systemic aspects of the family of origin, autonomy and intimacy in the student's family of origin, as well as rules, roles, rituals, and relationships. This assignment increases the students' awareness of the powerful impact of their families of origin, of what they have done so far to deal with "the unachieved goals and the unresolved problems" of previous generations, and of what they would like to do or change in their significant familial relationships in the present and the future. Piercy and Sprenkle (1984) noted that students often consider this paper a highlight in the family therapy graduate program.

CONCLUSION

In a course on family-of-origin issues, the first two objectives (i.e., understanding family-of-origin theory and learning techniques for use in family-of-origin work) usually present no difficulties, either for the students or for the teacher. More sensitive, however, is the third objective: personal work by students on their own family of origin. Braverman (1982) noted that the "dilemma for the teacher in doing family-of-origin work as a part of a training program is to find the boundary between teaching and doing therapy" (p. 629). In dealing with this dilemma, teachers of graduate courses in family-of-origin issues may well consider the following points:

1. Students need to know beforehand the requirements of the course.
2. It is essential to develop a high level of trust, both between student and teacher and among the students (Braverman, 1982).
3. Limitation of class size seems essential; classes with more than 15 students tend to become too "impersonal." The ideal number of students seems to be about 12. This number is small enough to allow trust to grow and large enough to reap the benefits of class interaction.
4. Sharing of personal family-of-origin work with the class should be *offered* by the student, not *required* by the teacher (Braverman, 1982).
5. Those who teach this class should have adequate clinical skills to deal with any problems that may arise for a student during or immediately after a class session (Braverman, 1982).
6. Teachers of this course should ask the students to do only what they themselves are willing to do. For example, they should have begun work on their own family-of-origin issues before attempting to teach such a course.

REFERENCES

Anderson, C., & Malloy, E. (1976). Family photographs in treatment and training. *Family Process, 15,* 259–264.

Bloomfield, H. (1983). *Making peace with your parents.* New York: Ballantine Books.

Boszormenyi-Nagy, I., & Ulrich, D. (1981). Contextual family therapy. In A.S. Gurman & D.P. Kniskern (Eds.), *Handbook of family therapy* (pp. 159–186). New York: Brunner/Mazel.

Bowen, M. (1978). *Family therapy in clinical practice.* New York: Jason Aronson.

Bradt, J.O. (1980). *The family diagram: Method, technique and use in family therapy.* Washington, DC: Groome Center.

Braverman, S. (1982). Family of origin as a training resource for family therapists. *Canadian Journal of Psychiatry, 27,* 629–633.

Bray, J., Williamson, D., & Malone, P. (1984). Personal authority in the family system: Development of a questionnaire to measure personal authority in intergenerational family processes. *Journal of Marital and Family Therapy, 10,* 167–178.

Constantine, L. (1978). Family sculpture and relationship mapping techniques. *Journal of Marriage and Family Counseling, 4,* 13–23.

Duhl, F., Kantor, D., & Duhl, B. (1973). Learning, space, and action in family therapy: A primer of sculpture. *Seminars in Psychiatry, 5,* 167–183.

Ford, F.R. (1983). Rules: The invisible family. *Family Process, 22,* 135–145.

Framo, J. (1976). Family of origin as a therapeutic resource for adults in marital therapy: You can and should go home again. *Family Process, 14,* 193–210.

Framo, J. (1981). The integration of marital therapy with sessions with family of origin. In A.S. Gurman & D.P. Kniskern (Eds.), *Handbook of family therapy.* New York: Brunner/Mazel.

Guerin, P.J., & Pendagast, E.G. (1976). Evaluation of family system and genogram. In P.J. Guerin (Ed.), *Family therapy.* New York: Gardner Press.

Hof, L., & Berman, E. (1986). The sexual genogram. *Journal of Marital and Family Therapy, 12,* 39–48.

Hovestadt, A., Anderson, W., Piercy, F., Cochran, S., & Fine, M. (1985). A family of origin scale. *Journal of Marital and Family Therapy, 11,* 287–298.

Jefferson, C. (1978). Some notes on the use of family sculpture in therapy. *Family Process, 17,* 69–76.

Jolly, W., Froom, J., & Rosen, M.G. (1980). The genogram. *Journal of Family Practice, 10,* 147–152.

Kramer, J.R. (1985). *Family interfaces: Transgenerational patterns.* New York: Brunner/Mazel.

Lewis, J., Beavers, W.R., Gosset, J., & Phillips, B. (1976). *No single thread.* New York: Brunner/Mazel.

Lieberman, S. (1979). Transgenerational analysis: The genogram as a technique in family therapy. *Journal of Family Therapy, 1,* 51–64.

McGoldrick, M., & Gerson, R. (1985). *Genograms in family assessment.* New York: W.W. Norton.

Napier, A.Y., & Whitaker, C.A. (1978). *The family crucible.* New York: Harper & Row.

Papp, P., Silverstein, O., & Carter, E. (1973). Family sculpting in preventive work with "well families." *Family Process, 12,* 197–212.

Piercy, F., & Sprenkel, D. (1984). The process of family therapy education. *Journal of Marital and Family Therapy, 10,* 399–408.

Simon, R.M. (1972). Sculpting the family. *Family Process, 2,* 149–157.

Wachtel, E. (1982). The family psyche over three generations: The genogram revisited. *Journal of Marital and Family Therapy, 8,* 335–343.

Whitaker, C., & Keith, D. (1981). Symbolic-experiential family therapy. In A.S. Gurman & D.P. Kniskern (Eds.), *Handbook of family therapy* (pp. 226–264). New York: Brunner/Mazel.

Williamson, D. (1978). New life at the graveyard: A method of therapy for individuation from a dead former parent. *Journal of Marriage and Family Counseling, 4,* 93–102.

Williamson, D. (1981). Personal authority via termination of the intergenerational hierarchical boundary: A "new" stage in the family life cycle. *Journal of Marital and Family Therapy, 7,* 441–452.

Williamson, D. (1982a). Personal authority via termination of the intergenerational hierarchical boundary: Part II. The consultation process and the therapeutic method. *Journal of Marital and Family Therapy, 8,* 23–38.

Williamson, D. (1982b). Personal authority in family experience via termination of the intergenerational hierarchical boundary: Part III. Personal authority defined, and the power of play in the change process. *Journal of Marital and Family Therapy, 8,* 309–324.

Wolin, S., & Bennett, L. (1984). Family rituals. *Family Process, 23,* 401–420.

Index

G

H

I

J

K

FAMILY THERAPY COLLECTIONS

Volume 1— *Values, Ethics, Legalities and the Family Therapist.* L. L'Abate (Ed.), 1982.

Volume 2— *Therapy with Remarriage Families.* Messinger (Ed.), 1982.

Volume 3— *Clinical Approaches to Family Violence.* L.R. Barnhill (Ed.), 1982.

Volume 4— *Diagnosis and Assessment in Family Therapy.* B.P. Keeney (Ed.), 1982.

Volume 5— *Sexual Issues in Family Therapy.* J.D. Woody and R.H. Woody (Eds.), 1983.

Volume 6— *Cultural Perspectives in Family Therapy.* C.J. Falicov (Ed.), 1983.

Volume 7— *Clinical Implications of the Family Life Cycle.* H.A. Liddle (Ed.), 1983.

Volume 8— *Death and Grief in the Family.* T.T. Frantz (Ed.), 1983.

Volume 9— *Family Therapy with School Related Problems.* B.F. Okun (Ed.), 1984.

Volume 10— *Perspectives on Work and the Family.* S.H. Cramer (Ed.), 1984.

Volume 11— *Families with Handicapped Members.* E. Imber Coppersmith (Ed.), 1984.

Volume 12— *Divorce and Family Mediation.* S.C. Grebe (Ed.), 1984.

Volume 13— *Health Promotion in Family Therapy.* J.R. Springer and R.H. Woody (Eds.), 1985.

Volume 14— *Stages: Patterns of Change Over Time.* D.C. Breunlin (Ed.), 1985.

Volume 15— *Integrating Research and Clinical Practice.* L.L. Andreozzi (Ed.), 1985.

Volume 16— *Women and Family Therapy.* M. Ault-Riché (Ed.), 1985.

Volume 17— *The Interface of Individual and Family Therapy.* S. Sugarman (Ed.), 1986.

Volume 18— *Treating Young Children in Family Therapy.* L. Combrinck-Graham (Ed.), 1986.

Volume 19— *Indirect Approaches in Family Therapy.* S. de Shazer and R. Kral (Eds.), 1986.

Volume 20— *Eating Disorders.* Jill Elka Harkaway (Ed.), 1987.

FORTHCOMING VOLUMES

Volume 22— *Stress and Family Therapy.* D. Rosenthal (Ed.), 1987.

Volume 23— *Single Parent Families.* M. Lindblad-Goldberg (Ed.), 1987.